Design Stays

LUSTER

EUROPE'S MOST INSPIRING HOTELS AND GUESTHOUSES
HANDPICKED BY PETITE PASSPORT

TEXT AND IMAGES
Pauline Egge

FINAL EDITING
Hadewijch Ceulemans

TRANSLATION
Sandy Logan

GRAPHIC DESIGN
Foreign Policy Design

Creative Director Yah-Leng Yu
Art Director Sylvester Tan
Designer Yun Xuan Lee
Illustrations Ying Xuan Loh

AUTHOR PHOTO
Alexander Santos Lima

D/2024/12.005/2
ISBN 9789460583612
NUR 500

© 2024 Luster Publishing, Antwerp
info@lusterpublishing.com
lusterpublishing.com
@lusterbooks

All rights reserved.
No part of this publication may be reproduced, stored in a retrieval system, or transmitted, in any form or by any means, without the prior written consent of the publisher. An exception is made for short excerpts, which may be cited for the sole purpose of reviews.

Since 2010, the year in which I launched *Petite Passport*, I can't help but feel butterflies in my stomach every time I check into a hotel and use my key card to open the door of the place I get to call my home for the night. Just like some people enjoy a sunset or the radiant colours of autumn foliage, I appreciate the beauty of a hotel room time and again. There's just something about the lack of clutter, the presence of meticulously curated design in the broadest sense of the word, and the anonymity which makes everything seem possible. At HOY in Paris, I get to become the yoga fanatic I aspire to be, whereas Los Enamorados in Ibiza inspires me to lead a more colourful life in every sense of the word.

Comments like 'Isn't a hotel room just for sleeping?' completely ignore the years the owner spent dreaming about this hotel, the architect's and/or the designer's process, and the commitment of the staff to ensure your experience is always memorable. What does it take to convert a former women's prison in Berlin into a hotel? How do you design and furnish a ski chalet in Switzerland without veering into clichés? What happens when a woman who worked in finance in Paris decides she is ready for a new challenge and teams up with the locals in Lagos to open one of the nicest hotels in Portugal? These stories deserve to be told, so I decided to write about the most inspiring design stays I have visited in recent years. All in Europe, in cities or in the countryside. They include high-end once-in-a-lifetime hotels (Pa.*te*.os near Lisbon, for example, see p. 222) but also more affordable* stays that are equally unique (such as the Warszauer in Kraków on p.122).

During my visits, I observed that hotels are gradually morphing into proper brands. Nowadays, almost every hotel has a shop where you can snap up some merchandise, like scented candles, honey from the hotel's hives, and hoodies and caps bearing the hotel's name. We like to show where we've stayed rather than reveal which brands we prefer to wear. There's more value in experiences than in owning stuff. And although sustainability used to be limited to solar panels, it is implemented on every level these days. Not building a swimming pool because the sea is nearby, organising a beach clean-up with locals and guests or – the cherry on the cake – offering a rental service for trendy ski apparel, which you can find in your room to avoid unnecessary purchases.

This book is a compilation of 14 years of travel, photography, and listening to all these inspiring stories, and it's my way of sharing all of my favourite hotels with people who love design and travel just as much as I do. People who may not have the time to spend two hours listening to an impassioned hotel owner, see seven different room types, and attempt to photograph the hotel lobby without people in the frame, but who do want to make the most of their stay. To all of you who feel your heart skipping a beat in anticipation when you walk to your hotel room, key card in hand: I wish you many pleasant stays and happy reading!

* Room prices start at under 200 euros in 20 of the 45 hotels.

Pauline Egge

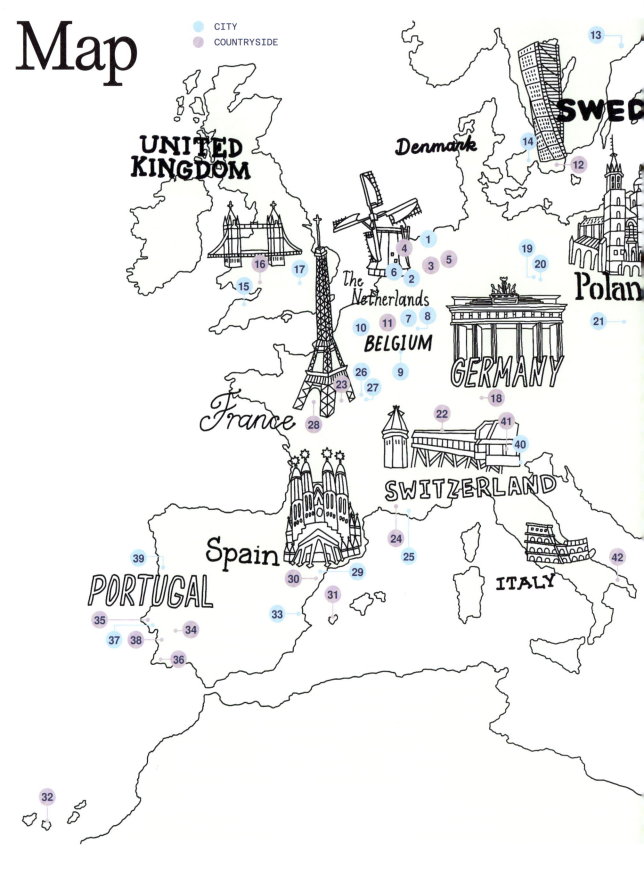

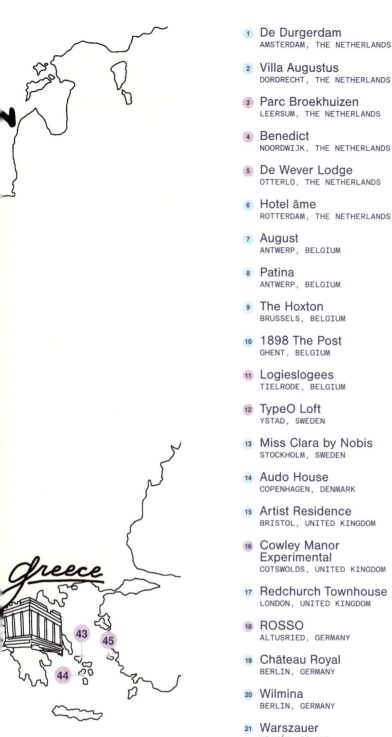

#	Name	Page
1	**De Durgerdam** — AMSTERDAM, THE NETHERLANDS	06
2	**Villa Augustus** — DORDRECHT, THE NETHERLANDS	12
3	**Parc Broekhuizen** — LEERSUM, THE NETHERLANDS	18
4	**Benedict** — NOORDWIJK, THE NETHERLANDS	24
5	**De Wever Lodge** — OTTERLO, THE NETHERLANDS	30
6	**Hotel âme** — ROTTERDAM, THE NETHERLANDS	36
7	**August** — ANTWERP, BELGIUM	42
8	**Patina** — ANTWERP, BELGIUM	48
9	**The Hoxton** — BRUSSELS, BELGIUM	54
10	**1898 The Post** — GHENT, BELGIUM	60
11	**Logieslogees** — TIELRODE, BELGIUM	64
12	**TypeO Loft** — YSTAD, SWEDEN	70
13	**Miss Clara by Nobis** — STOCKHOLM, SWEDEN	76
14	**Audo House** — COPENHAGEN, DENMARK	82
15	**Artist Residence** — BRISTOL, UNITED KINGDOM	88
16	**Cowley Manor Experimental** — COTSWOLDS, UNITED KINGDOM	92
17	**Redchurch Townhouse** — LONDON, UNITED KINGDOM	98
18	**ROSSO** — ALTUSRIED, GERMANY	104
19	**Chäteau Royal** — BERLIN, GERMANY	110
20	**Wilmina** — BERLIN, GERMANY	116
21	**Warszauer** — KRAKÓW, POLAND	122
22	**Experimental Chalet** — VERBIER, SWITZERLAND	128
23	**Le Barn** — BONNELLES, FRANCE	134
24	**Le Moulin** — LOURMARIN, FRANCE	140
25	**Tuba** — MARSEILLE, FRANCE	146
26	**Hotel HOY** — PARIS, FRANCE	152
27	**Le Pigalle** — PARIS, FRANCE	158
28	**D'une île** — RÉMALARD, FRANCE	164
29	**Casa Bonay** — BARCELONA, SPAIN	170
30	**Little Beach House** — GARRAF, SPAIN	176
31	**Los Enamorados** — IBIZA, SPAIN	182
32	**Casa de las Flores** — LANZAROTE, SPAIN	188
33	**Yours** — VALENCIA, SPAIN	194
34	**São Lourenço do Barrocal** — BARROCAL, PORTUGAL	198
35	**Marqí** — COLARES, PORTUGAL	204
36	**Casa Mãe** — LAGOS, PORTUGAL	210
37	**Santa Clara 1728** — LISBON, PORTUGAL	216
38	**Pa.te.os** — MELIDES, PORTUGAL	222
39	**Tipografia do Conto** — PORTO, PORTUGAL	228
40	**Parkhotel Mondschein** — BOLZANO, ITALY	234
41	**Villa Arnica** — LANA, ITALY	240
42	**Masseria Moroseta** — OSTUNI, ITALY	246
43	**The Wild Hotel** — MYKONOS, GREECE	252
44	**Parīlio** — PAROS, GREECE	258
45	**Casa Cook** — SAMOS, GREECE	264

(CITY)

De Durgerdam
Amsterdam, The Netherlands

06

Durgerdam is a quaint fishing village with a population of just 500 inhabitants, situated just outside of Amsterdam. Sandwiched between its blue-and-white houses lies a former village pub, which, in the 17th century, used to be an inn for fishermen. When the owner decided the pub was in need of refurbishing, he reached out to sustainable investment company Aedes. Although they were new to the hospitality industry, they were interested in the project on the condition that they would be able to work with the best of the best. And that's how the partnership with Buro Belén came about, a Dutch design studio known for its extensive materials research. The designers, who have been apprenticed to Ilse Crawford, began by researching the light, colours, and materials of 17th-century Holland and the Zuiderzee, incorporating their findings into hotel De Durgerdam and restaurant De Mark. The rusty red colour of the beams in the suites, for example, is inspired by the colour of the sails of 17th-century ships. The eye-catching plaids on the bed are made of a luxurious fabric that changes colour with the light, while *Lacrime del Pescatore* (fishermen's tears), the artwork by Ingo Maurer above the large dining table in the restaurant, is made from old fishing nets. The hotel has a few suites above the restaurant, which you reach via the centuries-old staircase, in addition to a few more spacious rooms in the garden behind the main building. All rooms are designed with the guests' comfort in mind, offering a place where you unwind the minute you sink into the soft sofa and sip a Durgerdammers Visser Borrel. The window seat in the largest suite has views of the IJmeer, making you wonder what it must have looked like here in the old days when people used to go skating on the lake, like in a painting by an old Dutch master. Michelin-starred chefs Richard van Oostenbrugge and Thomas Groot of 212** oversee De Mark's soulful menu, which includes several classics such as tomato tartare and cod. The restaurant is as popular with locals who don't feel like cooking as with, for example, couples looking to celebrate their fifth wedding anniversary. In winter you can eat inside, where a fire is crackling in the cosy fireplace, and sheepskins adorn the chairs. In summer, nothing beats the al fresco dining experience on the terrace. You can take a cooling dip in the water or clear your mind during a walk along the dyke on a rainy autumn day wearing one of the custom-made KASSL Editions raincoats provided by the hotel.

BEST ROOM:
The first-floor suite overlooking the water, where you sleep in a cosy nook and there's a free-standing bathtub.

NEARBY:
Restaurant Vuurtoreneiland is housed in a glasshouse on a private island that you can only reach by boat. In winter, they open the doors of their winter restaurant.

TAKE HOME:
The KASSL jackets aren't for sale at the hotel, but you can always buy one afterwards and enjoy the memories whenever you wear it.

SUSTAINABLE EFFORTS:
There's a Hydraloop, an innovative system that recycles shower water so it can be used to flush toilets and water the garden.

DE DURGERDAM

Durgerdammerdijk 73 Amsterdam
www.dedurgerdam.com

FROM 305 euro A NIGHT

DE DURGERDAM

CITY

Villa Augustus
Dordrecht, The Netherlands

12

When you arrive at Villa Augustus, it feels like you've reached an oasis of refinement. The vegetable garden is in full bloom, the water of the Wantij ripples gently in the wind, and the Limonaia, a greenhouse where lemon trees are kept from November to April, becomes a pop-up restaurant in summer. The garden was voted 'Garden of the Year' by the English magazine *Gardens Illustrated* a few years ago, which is all the more remarkable because no non-English garden had ever won this award. Villa Augustus is built around a water tower, where some of the hotel rooms are located, but there is also an old pump building in the grounds, which has been converted into a restaurant. The restaurant's fabulous afternoon tea, presented on a tiered tray full of filled sourdough rolls, scones with clotted cream and other sweets, draws guests from all over the country, if not the world. The restaurant is also open for breakfast, lunch, and dinner, using produce from its vegetable garden where possible. The shop next to the restaurant stocks anything from a good book to gardening tools, flowers, a linen apron or tasty produce. Dorine de Vos (of restaurant Loos and Hotel New York in Rotterdam) designed the interior and also created the cheerful illustrations of the hare throughout the hotel. The hotel rooms are scattered around the property. You can sleep in the water tower with panoramic views and its many historical details, such as the headboards of the beds, which are made from old machine doors. The Lantern Room is popular with newlyweds because of its sweeping views. On clear days, you can even see the Euromast in Rotterdam in the distance. The floating rooms, situated on a 1903 office ship that overlooks the Wantij, are a more recent addition, with the sound of gently lapping water in the background. The garden rooms give out on the garden, ensuring you can wake up in the morning and step out into the vegetable garden when all is still nice and quiet. The very soft linens on the bed guarantee a good night's sleep. From Villa Augustus, you can take the water bus to Rotterdam, explore friendly Dordrecht, or take a walk through the Biesbosch – who knows, you might even spot a beaver!

VILLA AUGUSTUS

BEST ROOM:
The floating rooms overlooking the Wantij.

NEARBY:
Hazel is a lovely café in Dordrecht. Do order the pistachio-and-chocolate biscuits.

TAKE HOME:
Fresh antipasti, their homemade granola and a recipe notebook with drawings by Dorine de Vos.

SUSTAINABLE EFFORTS:
From early spring through winter, the gardener and the chef pick seasonal vegetables from the organic vegetable garden.

www.villa-augustus.nl
Oranjelaan 7
Dordrecht
<< DESIGN STAYS >>

FROM
125 euro
A NIGHT

(COUNTRYSIDE)

Parc Broekhuizen

Leersum, The Netherlands

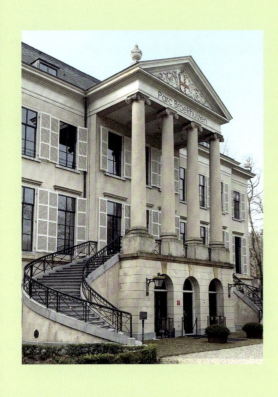

18

BEST ROOM:
The Terrace Suite with its large terrace and cosy bedroom.

NEARBY:
Utrecht is just 30 minutes by car, but you can also take lovely long walks in the surrounding area.

TAKE HOME:
Honey from Broekhuizen's apiary.

DON'T MISS:
They regularly organise exhibitions in Parc Broekhuizen and the surrounding park.

Parc Broekhuizen is a hotel and culinary destination in one, located on a country estate in the forests of Leersum near Utrecht. The arrival says it all: as you drive up the avenue surrounded by trees, you can already spot the white castle where Parc Broekhuizen opened its doors in 2016 in the distance. The castle's history dates back to the 14th century, after which several noble families lived there. In the 20th century, the building was used by the Dutch Ministry of Agriculture and Fisheries. After remaining vacant for years, the property was finally renovated and designer Judith van Mourik was hired to create a contemporary interior, with respect and love for the building's history. One of the first-floor rooms has hand-painted wallpapers on canvas by Willem Joseph Laguy dating from 1780, while a contemporary chandelier by Jan Pauwels hangs in the stairwell. Check out the colour gradient stair runner, designed by Van Mourik, and inspired by a haute couture dress, which gradually changes colour. Parc Broekhuizen has rooms and suites in the main building and in the former coach house. All the rooms are different. Some have a rather standard interior, but the Terrace Suite, Panorama Suite and the Grand Suite are definitely worth booking. The first suite has a large terrace, a cosy bedroom, and a freestanding bathtub. The Panorama Suite still has the original wood panelling, adding to the warm atmosphere. And the Grand Suite has phenomenal views of the lake and forests. The intention was always to make Parc Broekhuizen a culinary destination. When they opened restaurant Voltaire on the ground floor, they were able to hire none other than three Michelin-starred chef Jacob Jan Boerma. Within two years of the restaurant's opening, it was awarded a Michelin star. These days, the menu is in hands of chef Arturo Dalhuisen, who has received praise for his bold flavours. The barn on the estate has been converted into a more accessible restaurant called Bistro Lof. Here chef Ewout Eleveld, who worked with Boerma for 17 years, serves tasty family dishes, presented on stylish tableware, with the pizzette (with baba ganoush with white cheese, for example) being especially popular. Where possible, the chefs source ingredients from their own vegetable garden, adjacent to the sunny terrace. A good starting or ending point for a walk in the area.

FROM 235 euro A NIGHT

Broekhuizerlaan 2
Leersum
www.parcbroekhuizen.nl

PARC BROEKHUIZEN

(COUNTRYSIDE)

Benedict

Noordwijk, The Netherlands

24

BEST ROOM:
The Benedict Loft is the biggest and most beautiful room, but the Superior Studios are highly recommended as well: here you sleep under a pitched roof and there's a Togo by Ligne Roset to enjoy the view over Noordwijk and the sea.

NEARBY:
Tulum is a fantastic beach club. Noordwijk is also very popular with kite surfers.

TAKE HOME:
Frama hand soap, handmade linen tea towels, and organic wine from the hotel's shop.

SUSTAINABLE EFFORTS:
The water pump that cools and heats each of the apartments and studios with fresh and healthy outdoor air.

Noordwijk aan Zee is an upmarket seaside resort on the North Sea coast where the elite have been flocking to for decades to benefit from the sea's healing effects. The European Spa Association (ESA) even officially declared it a 'European Spa Destination' because of the excellent, healthy quality of its seawater, air and nature. Boutique hotel Benedict is happy to contribute to this reputation, fitting each of its apartments with a top-notch sustainable water pump that allows healthy outdoor air to continuously enter the rooms, in addition to conventional air conditioning or heating. Some hotels flaunt these types of gadgets, but here guests really *feel* the difference: the air in the rooms is so fresh that you'd think you're the first to stay there. The hotel's passion for sustainability is palpable everywhere you look: there's solar panels and triple glazing, and they use a natural cleaning product that kills 99.9% of bacteria, in order to maintain a plastic- and toxin-free environment. Of course the look of the hotel matters too, and indeed the design has certainly been taken more than care of. The entire building has a serene ambience thanks to a soft colour palette. The owners, who prefer to remain anonymous, partnered with designer Paul Linse of Studio Linse. While all the apartments are different, they all have a kitchenette, interesting artwork, a nice bed, and hand soap from Danish brand Frama. There are cosy love nests, as well as apartments with beds for up to six guests. The Deluxe Apartment has a bunk bed for children and a clawfoot tub, while the Studio is smaller but has soothing green views and a balcony. Benedict's Loft is the most luxurious option, with 60m^2 of space and a view of the tulip fields from the freestanding bathtub and the beach from the balcony. Benedict is located in a residential neighbourhood, just a ten-minute walk to the beach. Tulum, one of the nicest beach clubs in the Netherlands, is a little further away; it's nice to know that the hotel has electric bikes available to guests. If you don't mind travelling a little further afield, visiting Museum Voorlinden, a private museum with a wonderful modern and contemporary art collection and a beautiful sculpture garden, is highly recommended. You can get there in under 30 minutes by car.

(COUNTRYSIDE)

De Wever Lodge
Otterlo, The Netherlands

30

Rogier van der Meer and Floris Rost van Tonningen wanted to open a hotel in the Netherlands centred around silence, nature and craft, but they had no idea where. So they travelled up and down the country searching for the right place. One day, they happened upon the outdated Carnegie Cottage in Otterlo, frequented by a target group of over-60s for the most part, who liked to stop in for the apple pie with whipped cream and the superb views of the Veluwe nature reserve. The owner at the time happened to be on the verge of retirement, which is how De Wever Lodge was born. The building needed a bit of a refresh, so Van der Meer and Rost van Tonningen asked the architects at Framework to renovate the hotel and restaurant completely, considering the property's history and surroundings. The colour palette is in tune with the colours of the surrounding nature, they used sand from the Veluwe for the stucco in the rooms, and they worked with local craftsmen for the furnishings. Above all, the owners wanted the hotel to exude a sense of serenity, ensuring guests would immediately feel relaxed when they arrive. And how could you not feel relaxed when you park your car and realise that the Veluwe is right there, just steps away. Inhaling the fresh air of nature has precisely the same effect as an expensive scented candle, especially in autumn. Adirondack chairs are arranged around a campfire on the terrace in front of De Wever Lodge. Inside, in the conservatory, apple pie with whipped cream is still on the menu, although patrons now tend to focus more on the interior with lounge sofas and sheepskins. It has become a popular spot where hikers like to give their feet a rest, and guests order lunch. There's also the restaurant, where the chef cooks with local ingredients, and where the vibe is slightly warmer thanks to custom wooden furniture made by a local carpenter and a lovely lounge sofa that invites you to sit down with one of the books from the bookcase or play a game. You have a choice of 14 rooms and two cottages. While the smallest room (Cosy) is not very spacious with its sloping ceiling, it is very snug and overlooks the heath. At the other end of the spectrum is the Charm Suite, which offers the same view and has a freestanding bathtub. They now also rent out black wooden cottages, one of which used to be a painter's cottage, if you and your family need a break in nature.

FROM 175 euro A NIGHT

Onderlangs 35
Otterlo
www.weverlodge.nl

BEST ROOM:
The Charm Suite with freestanding bathtub and spacious terrace overlooking the countryside.

NEARBY:
The Veluwe is the most beautiful nature park in the Netherlands. The Kröller-Müller Museum, with works by Van Gogh and Mondrian, is nestled in the heart of the forest.

TAKE HOME:
Manalo's sticky chai tea.

DON'T MISS:
Join shepherd Jeroen to learn more about the craft of sheep herding. You can also choose to visit a gin distiller, beekeeper, baker, hunter or artist.

CITY

Hotel âme
Rotterdam, The Netherlands

36

If you don't know there is a hotel, café, and shop behind the white façade in Eendrachtsweg in Rotterdam, you'd walk right past it. But the connecting road between the city centre and bustling Witte de Withstraat on one side and Depot Boijmans Van Beuningen, the Nieuwe Instituut and the Kunsthal on the other, is home to a hotel with a warm minimalist feel. Angel Kwok currently runs the hotel after a major renovation of this listed building from 1867 that previously housed Michelin-starred restaurant De Engel. The original interior was all about black chandeliers, gold-rimmed mirrors, and lots of dark wood throughout. After the building was stripped, daylight now pours in from both sides, the café has a hushed pink bar, and light brown tables and chairs. Lots of the furniture was custom-made for the hotel, but Kwok also works with design brands such as TAKT, 101 Copenhagen, and Muller Van Severen. The hotel's name comes from the French word *âme*, meaning soul. The property's soul comes to life by preserving the old and pairing it with inspiration from Scandinavia and Japan – countries the owner loves to visit. In the café, hotel guests mix with locals who like to drop in for a coffee, with or without a freshly baked canelé. In the shop on the same floor, the owner sells her ceramics and other brands she finds inspiring. The range includes notebooks by Rotterdam-based graphic designer Marjolein Delhaas and coffee accessories by Japanese brand KINTO. The bedrooms are serene retreats. The smallest room, Petite, has only a bed and a small bathroom, but the large window overlooks

DESIGN STAYS

BEST ROOM:
Monumental+ with a blissful bath.

NEARBY:
Depot Boijmans Van Beuningen restaurant Renilde, and Susan Bijl's flagshipstore are all within walking distance.

TAKE HOME:
Studio Kurē's limited edition ceramics.

SUSTAINABLE EFFORTS:
The hotel's Coco-mat beds are handmade and 100% natural.

Boijmans Van Beuningen and Franz West's artworks on Westersingel. Perfect for solo travellers. Monumental+ is the largest suite with a high ceiling, atmospheric linen curtains, and a freestanding bathtub. If you prefer fresh air during your stay, the Garden Room has a private garden. Besides sleeping, eating and shopping, you can also learn new skills in the hotel. Past events include a Japanese kirie workshop where children mastered the Japanese paper cutting technique with their parents and a shio-koji ceremonial workshop to make your own Japanese fermented flavouring.

HOTEL ÂME

FROM 109 euro A NIGHT

Eendrachtsweg 19
Rotterdam
www.hotelame.com

41   HOTEL ÂME

(CITY)

August
Antwerp, Belgium

42

BEST ROOM:
The Experience Plus room, with its centuries-old wooden ceiling and clawfoot tub. The most romantic option.

NEARBY:
Restaurant The Jane.

TAKE HOME:
The room spray with August's tailor-made fragrance.

SUSTAINABLE EFFORTS:
The natural swimming pool and the herb garden where the chef picks the herbs for his dishes.

't Groen Kwartier is a creative urban district of close to eight hectares centred around a former military hospital. Michelin-starred restaurant The Jane is located in the old chapel, there is a 1,200-m² urban agriculture project on the rooftops of PAKT and, in 2019, hotel August opened its doors in the former Augustinian convent. This is the second hotel project of entrepreneur Mouche Van Hool, who also runs Hotel Julien. Together with Belgian architect Vincent Van Duysen, she converted the old convent into a hotel with 44 rooms, a restaurant, bar, spa, several meeting rooms, and a shop across the street. The hushed colours, timeless furniture, and windows with a view of the renovated monastery and green garden exude tranquillity, so that as a guest you're naturally inclined to slow down and unwind. This is the perfect modern-day sanctuary. Whether you stay in one of the former convent rooms, treat yourself to a hot bath at the end of the day in one of the rooms under the centuries-old beamed ceiling, or sleep in the extra-spacious August Suite: all the rooms have beds made with Egyptian percale linens and Le Labo toiletries in the bathroom. It only takes ten minutes by bike to get from the hotel to the city centre, but of course you can just stay in and book the spa instead, in which case the intimate wellness area is reserved exclusively for you. Book a massage or facial, visit the hammam, cool down with fresh ice scrubs, or take a lovely dip in the pool. The spa is also open to non-guests by the way, as are the restaurant and bar. Nick Bril, the chef of The Jane, also oversees August's restaurant, ensuring both the lunch and dinner menus focus on seasonal produce. For dinner, you can choose from a four- or five-course menu featuring creative dishes with top-class ingredients like Piemontese beef or black truffle. Last but definitely not least, there's the most impressive and most photographed space in the hotel: the bar in the former chapel. The space has been completely renovated of course, but the marble on the walls, the stained-glass windows, and the striking tiles are all authentic. Here the menu features cocktails, wine and some finger food. The Bloody Mary by Nick Bril, also available in a virgin version, is a nod to the former occupants: we are, after all, in a historic convent.

Jules Bordetstraat 5
Antwerp
www.august-antwerp.com

FROM
209 euro
A NIGHT

Patina

Antwerp, Belgium

48

Lies Mertens established her sustainable bag label in 2017 and now has two boutiques in Antwerp and Brussels. Her dream was always to have a studio, gallery, and guesthouse under one roof and when she was house hunting in Antwerp, she found a house where the artist Rinus Van de Velde had also lived and worked. Although one section was in need of a major refurbishment, there was also a new building on the site, with a patio overgrown with ivy, and a rooftop terrace on the first floor. The perfect place for a gallery. Mertens has already hosted several shows there, which have a great side effect, seeing that the artists are more than happy to showcase their designs, knowledge, and skills in the apartments that she installed in the front house. The artist Katie Tomlinson has created a work especially for Patina (with one of Mertens's bags in a cameo), there is an aluminium lamp by Pieter Nyssen, and designers Iona Tettelin and Astrid Venlet helped furnish the guesthouse, which has two apartments and a shared kitchen and dining room. The rooms are very spacious and full of creative and unusual solutions. Mertens did a lot herself. Her Dutch uncle made the bed frame, which she then covered with scraps of leather, creating another work of art in the process. The bathroom wall is clad with waste from a construction site, converted into a sustainable clay building material by BC Materials. And to insulate and soundproof the second-floor room, they opted for carpet to cover the floor, extending it onto the bed frame. Apparently guests find this upper room so comfy that they are happy to stay in for the entire day. There's also a book case, with lots of choices, which you can read while laying on the daybed in front of the window. The interior is a mix of designer furniture that Mertens collected in the past years and items that were custom-made by designers she knows. Other details also stand out: guests can pamper their skin with the lovely sustainable skincare line of Belgian brand Maiwe. As you head out to explore the lively 't Groen Kwartier, you may catch a glimpse of the designer herself, at work in her groundfloor studio.

BEST ROOM:
Room 2 if you like books. There are over 1,000 books in the cabinet.

NEARBY:
Nives in nearby Harmonie Park serves a great lunch.

TAKE HOME:
Are you in the market for a new weekend bag? Consider buying Lies Mertens's Ed online for your next trip.

SUSTAINABLE EFFORTS:
They reused the hundreds of Winckelmans tiles they found in the cellar for the bathrooms, dining room, and kitchen.

www.patina-antwerp.be
Albert Grisarstraat 52
Antwerp
DESIGN STAYS
FROM 165 euro A NIGHT

The Hoxton
Brussels, Belgium

54

It all started just after the opening of the very first Hoxton Hotel in Shoreditch in London with the infamous £1 room sale. People sat at their computers, endlessly clicking refresh in hopes of scoring a room for this cheap price, as if they were trying to buy coveted tickets to a Beyonce concert. The Hoxton promoted itself as an affordable boutique hotel in one of London's coolest neighbourhoods. A radically new approach in a market that was largely dominated by impersonal, massive hotel chains. It attracted a mix of creative minds, travellers who wanted to be surprised and also locals, which was quite new at the time. Even today, this is an important part of their philosophy. All their hotels have a bustling lobby with a restaurant that is open to locals and guests alike, but they also hire local artists and designers to fill the shelves of the Hox Shop with their wares and create art for the walls. Given that they now have 15 branches (including three in the United States), the hotel could also be categorised as a

chain, albeit a unique one. No hotel is the same. They are all key destinations in a city, attracting a fun mix of people of all ages who like an affordable hotel room. The Hoxton in Brussels opened its doors in 2023 in the Victoria Tower, the former IBM headquarters near the Botanique city park. Once inside, the smell of freshly baked chocolate peanut butter biscuits wafts towards you from the coffee bar and you can already see the hotel's spectacular living room in the distance. The bar is one floor lower and features comfortable seating with a ledge full of plants above it, and four eye-catching lamps by Santa & Cole. Also on this floor is Cantina Valentina, a Peruvian-inspired restaurant with a breakfast menu that includes açai bowls, quinoa pancakes and avocado toast. Restaurant Tope, on the 22nd floor, is highly recommended, if only for the panoramic view of the city from the terrace, with chic red and white parasols and great Mexican tacos and cocktails. For the interior of the rooms, they took inspiration from the 1970s with wooden accents, pink bathroom furniture, and a frosted-glass room divider. They are also located on the upper floors of the hotel, from where you look out over a city that never seems to stop.

BEST ROOM:
The Biggy is the largest room, but the Roomy Bath has a bathtub with a view.

NEARBY:
Not necessarily around the corner, but Nightshop is just a 30-minute walk from The Hoxton. A great spot for a cider and sharing plates.

TAKE HOME:
You can buy the bum bag from Belgian fashion brand Bellerose in the Hox Shop.

SUSTAINABLE EFFORTS:
They reused tiles from the old building in the new interior design.

FROM 209 euro A NIGHT

www.thehoxton.com
Square Victoria Régina 1
Brussels

THE HOXTON

CITY

1898
The Post

Ghent, Belgium

60

BEST ROOM:
The Letter with its high ceilings, views of Korenmarkt, and thick curtains for even deeper sleep.

NEARBY:
Design Museum Gent is just a five-minute walk from the hotel. It closed its doors in 2023 because of a large renovation, including a brand new wing. The reopening is planned for 2026. In the meantime you can visit Ding Vitrine, a small pop-up exhibition space and info point for the museum's extramural exhibitions. For the best coffee in town, head to Way Coffee Roasters. Don't forget to check out the first floor if you like (cook) books.

TAKE HOME:
The postcards, which you can also post to loved ones in the hotel.

SUSTAINABLE EFFORTS:
The hotel uses wooden reusable boxes for their gift vouchers.

DON'T MISS:
In summer, enjoy oysters and champagne on the outdoor terrace overlooking the River Lys.

FROM 179 euro A NIGHT
www.1898thepost.com
Graslei 16
Ghent

One of the most beautiful photos you can take of Ghent is from the famous Sint-Michiels bridge. From here you have a view of Graslei, where you can watch the occasional tourist boat sail past and where locals like to meet up along the quay. This charming setting is where you'll find the 1898 The Post. The stately building was designed by Louis Cloquet, who's also the architect of the Sint-Michiels bridge. If you don't realise this former post office is now home to a hotel, it's easy to walk past its façade without noticing the entrance. Once you've found it, and have taken the lift or the spiral staircase to the reception desk, you can start exploring all that 1898 The Post has to offer. Everything in the hotel refers to the history of the building, a former mail sorting centre where the mail for the people of Ghent and beyond was sorted for over 100 years. The hotel's smallest room is called the Stamp, but you can also stay in the Letter, Envelope or Carriage. Interestingly, the room type called 'the Carriage with a Private Terrace', which overlooks Korenmarkt, is dedicated to the former postmaster. The room interiors are classic, with lots of wood, dark green walls, and long, heavy curtains. The homely details make the rooms feel even more luxurious: a chaise longue in front of the window from where you can watch life in the city take its course, Guerlain shower gel in the bathroom, and a postcard and pen ready for you to write a letter home. The hotel also has a bar, where a lavish breakfast is served with fresh juice, bowls full of fruit, fresh yoghurt with granola, pancakes, and a full omelette. And because the hotel is so centrally located, you can hit the city centre right after breakfast, ready for a stroll through the historic streets, a visit to one of Ghent's museums or some shopping at stylish boutiques like Twiggy. Back at the hotel, the bartenders at The Cobbler are only too happy to pour you a (non-alcoholic) cocktail. Nestle yourself in one of the comfy window seats to see Graslei from a different perspective: you'll probably want to seize the opportunity to take the second most beautiful photo of Ghent. Cheers!

1898 THE POST

| COUNTRYSIDE |

Logieslogees
Tielrode, Belgium

BEST ROOM:
Doorzicht, with its wonderful tub for a soothing bath at the end of the day.

NEARBY:
Book an Art-Deco walk in Sint-Niklaas to see some 20th-century architectural masterpieces.

TAKE HOME:
Handmade ceramics.

SUSTAINABLE EFFORTS:
The solar-powered hot water heater means you don't need a lot of wood to heat the hot tub.

Logieslogees is in Tielrode, a village in East Flanders, where urban dwellers soon unwind when they see the surrounding nature. You can follow a nine-kilometre hiking trail that takes you past a unique freshwater tidal area and through a nature reserve on paved and unpaved paths. But Tielrode is also a short drive to Sint-Niklaas, Ghent, and Antwerp. Logieslogees started out as Arck, short for architects' rooms. The architect couple who also lived and worked here designed the building. When the first owners moved out in 2022, graphic designer and goldsmith Kirsten Raes took over, together with her husband. They didn't just fall for the building, but also for the view and picturesque Tielrode. The couple left the design as is, adding a personal touch to the breakfast with lots of homemade food. The house has three rooms, called Inzicht, Uitzicht, and Doorzicht, with different colour schemes and varying levels of luxury. Inzicht is a dark room on the ground floor, whereas Uitzicht has crisp white walls and a Japandi-style interior. Light falls in from both sides in Doorzicht, the most luxurious room with a spacious bathroom, bathtub, and private terrace. The colour palette is inspired by the surrounding nature, so lots of wood tones and plants. The house overlooks Paardenpolder, a green nature reserve you can enjoy while sitting in the garden. The garden is also home to one of the unique selling points of Logieslogees: the hot tub by sustainable outdoor design brand Weltevree. Here you can enjoy the warm water in complete privacy while sipping some wine and counting the endless stars under a full moon. Besides your room, the house also has a communal breakfast area and an honesty bar with wine, local beer and other goodies. And thanks to the large windows, you can still enjoy your natural surroundings, even on bad weather days. Four-legged friends are also welcome (only in Inzicht), so you can combine a design stay with long walks with your dog.

FROM
135 euro
A NIGHT

www.logieslogees.be
Kaaistraat 23
Tielrode
<< DESIGN STAYS >>

DESIGN STAYS

(COUNTRYSIDE)

TypeO Loft

Ystad, Sweden

70

TypeO Loft is a one-room bed and breakfast in the hilly landscape of Skåne, Sweden's southernmost province. It's a 45-minute drive by car from Copenhagen to Magnus Wittbjer and Micha van Dinther's refurbished farmhouse from 1842, which they moved into in 2015 after years of living and working in Stockholm and Malmö. In Stockholm, they started TypeO, a website on which they sell furniture, accessories, and books that tickle their fancy, from ceramics by Hasami Porcelain from Japan and cushions by Read the Label. Once they found their footing in the countryside, they decided to transform part of their house into TypeO Loft, a place to stay and discover many of the products they sell on their website. This is anything but a rigid showroom setting because you can literally try everything, from Boiida tea towels for washing the dishes to a Hario V60 Ceramic Dripper and even the blissful skincare products from Swedish brand OM-SE. As a result, the loft feels more like a home than a hotel. All the more so because, next to the luxurious bed by Swedish brand Dux, you have access to a kitchen, small dining table, bathroom and spacious seating area with two Togo sofas by Ligne Roset to do some reading on rainy days. However, looking up from your book now and then is highly recommended as the panoramic view has the same effect as a meditative film. Here, showers, rainbows, clouds and birds (even the occasional red kite!) drift by. On sunny days, you can move to the spacious balcony with a relaxed corner sofa and a table where a sumptuous breakfast awaits when you arrive, including local products such as fresh fruit, cheese, jam, eggs, bread, and fresh apple juice. TypeO Loft makes you feel calmer the minute you arrive. It's an invitation to indulge in some *dolce far niente*, although there is plenty to explore nearby. Starting with Skåne's vast landscape dotted with rustling wheat fields and farmhouses, some of which have been transformed into a cool café (as is the case at Örum119). If you like beaches (Sandhammaren), Italian food (Pastafabriken) and art (Kivik Art Centre, open from June till October), this is the place to be.

NEARBY:
Swedish celebrity chef Daniel Berlin has opened a restaurant, bar, and hotel, about a 50-minute drive from TypeO Loft.

TAKE HOME:
OM-SE's Facial Cleansing Oil is renowned for its deep cleansing action.

SUSTAINABLE EFFORTS:
They work with local products where possible and use eco-friendly cleaning products.

www.typeo.se
Gamla Lundavägen 418 Ystad
FROM 230 euro A NIGHT

(CITY)

Miss Clara by Nobis

Stockholm, Sweden

76

One of Stockholm's most beautiful Art Nouveau buildings is situated along Sveavägen, the city's famous thoroughfare. Now a hotel, it formerly was a girls' school, of which Miss Clara was the headmistress. So, choosing a name was easy when they decided to open a hotel here in 2013. Miss Clara by Nobis belongs to the exclusive Nobis Hospitality Group, known for Nobis Hotel in Stockholm and Copenhagen, but whose portfolio also includes Concepció by Nobis in Mallorca and Blique by Nobis in Stockholm. These days there is not much to indicate that there used to be a school here, although the stairwell dates from that era and one of the Etage Suites was once the girls' prayer room.

DESIGN STAYS

Nobis collaborated with award-winning Swedish architect Gert Wingårdh for the interior, who also designed Magasin 211 in Malmö (with the fantastic restaurant Aster) and restaurant Freya in Stockholm. Most materials, including the wood the unique bed is made of, were sourced from Sweden. Comfortable seating seems to be a theme in the hotel rooms. The frame of the Thonet chair at the foot of the bed invites you to a face-to-face with your travelling companion, and even the smallest room also has a window seat where you can dream away while taking in the typical Stockholm views. In the Deluxe room there's also a chaise longue, while the suites have an entire living room. So if you decide to explore the city on foot, you'll definitely have plenty of space to stretch your legs afterwards. In some of the suites and in the Ballerina Room (meeting venue) on the ground floor, the ballerina photographs by photographer Max Modén catch the eye.

The street-side restaurant is open all day, serving classic international dishes such as vitello tonnato and chicken paillard. More recently, they opened a Neapolitan pizzeria next door, where hotel guests can also order drinks at the bar. Stockholm is the Scandinavian shopping city par excellence. Acne Studios, Hope, Byredo: these top Swedish brands are all here, and conveniently within walking distance. Don't forget to check out Södermalm district on the other side of the city as well, for Nitty Gritty, Papercut, Konstig Konstbokhandel, and Drop Coffee for the best coffee in town.

MISS CLARA

BEST ROOM:
The window seat in the Deluxe Room overlooks Sveavägen.

NEARBY:
Banacado is a vegan breakfast and brunch spot within walking distance.

TAKE HOME:
Bal d'Afrique shower gel by Byredo, the hotel's fragrance line.

SUSTAINABLE EFFORTS:
The hotel's orbital showers save as much as 80 % on water use.

FROM 235 euro A NIGHT
www.missclarahotel.com
Sveavägen 48
Stockholm

MISS CLARA

Audo House

Copenhagen, Denmark

82

What happens when Danish design brand Audo Copenhagen partners with Norm Architects and Kinfolk Magazine founder Nathan Williams to open a hotel? The result is Audo House. Jonas Bjerre-Poulsen of Norm Architects explains how he was inspired by the buzz at the Ace Hotel in New York, which has many different functions under one roof. They wanted to create something similar, but on a much smaller scale, and with a Scandinavian touch. Audo Copenhagen's offices share the building with a café, restaurant, concept store, and ten suites. Hotel guests sitting down for a typical Danish pastry and a specialty coffee in the morning will see the stylish Audo Copenhagen employees walking in and out. The architects wanted to shift away from white, almost sterile interiors to introduce what they call 'soft minimalism': pared-down yet warm interiors where all your senses are pampered in the best possible way. Anyone who has stayed here remembers the scent of the wood they use in the rooms months later. The colours are warm, the beds thick and comfy, and the Japanese-style bathroom is hidden in a closet. 'Audo' is short for *Ab Uno Disce Omnes*, Latin for 'From One Learn All', so they regularly invite artists, chefs, and other creative entrepreneurs for exhibitions, pop-up residencies, and workshops. The photos for example feature the work of American artist Benjamin Ewing, and in the past they teamed up with cool plant shop Plant København to organise a workshop for children teaching them how to grow plants. The Audo Concept Shop also sells work by (local) entrepreneurs whose work they admire, in addition to Audo Copenhagen's latest collection, that goes without saying. The in-house restaurant is open all day, for a freshly brewed coffee, a seasonal lunch and tasty dinner dishes like blue oyster mushrooms or octopus with fried cornmeal, made from local, organic ingredients, and served in a casual, minimalist chic setting. The Audo is located in Nordhavn, just 15 minutes by metro from the city centre. The port district, home to many design studios, is also the place to be if you're into sports. There is a rooftop gym on a car park, and you can swim in the harbour pool up the road.

BEST ROOM:
The studio rooms are the ultimate *hygge* destination with a Japanese-style bathroom hidden in a beautiful wooden closet.

NEARBY:
Hija de Sanchez Taquería for the best Mexican tacos and Andersen and Maillard Bakery for the best croissants.

TAKE HOME:
A print by Atelier CPH and the Midnight Soak scented candle by Audo Copenhagen.

SUSTAINABLE EFFORTS:
They only use refillable cosmetics, the bar in your room is stocked with local products, and the beds have duvet covers from sustainable Danish brand Aiayu.

FROM
375 euro
A NIGHT

Århusgade 130
Copenhagen
www.audocph.com

85 AUDO HOUSE

DESIGN STAYS

(CITY)

Artist Residence

Bristol, United Kingdom

88

BEST ROOM:
The Artist Suite, if only for the boudoir, where you can treat yourself to a facial after a leisurely bath.

NEARBY:
Head to Spike Island and the Spike Island gallery to see some modern art or check out Banksy's Girl with the Pearl Earring.

TAKE HOME:
An umbrella that was specially designed for the hotel in collaboration with HOWE.

SUSTAINABLE EFFORTS:
At the Artist Residence, the aim is always to repair rather than replace something. The bathroom is stocked with vegan and cruelty-free skincare products by Bramley. The chef incorporates locally sourced ingredients into the menu where possible.

The Artist Residence's genesis reads like a true success story: after graduating, owner Justin Salisbury went to help his parents with their bed and breakfast in Brighton, and got bitten by the hospitality-bug. With a minimal budget but a great love for art, he asked local artists to create artwork for the hotel, eventually rebranding it as the Artist Residence. He could have left it at that, but soon branches in Penzance, Bristol, Oxfordshire, and London followed. By then his wife Charlie Salisbury had come on board. Together they stumbled upon a former boot factory in St Paul's, a creative district in Bristol with a strong community vibe within walking distance of the city centre. An annual highlight in the area is the St Paul's Carnival in June, a Caribbean carnival that attracts thousands of people. The hotel, which opened its doors at the end of 2021, had so much potential that they decided to retain as many original details as possible, supplementing this with industrial and vintage furniture and, of course, lots of art. The hotel's 11 rooms are all different. The Shoebox is the smallest room, but lots of light falls in through the large window, making it seem much more spacious. The Artist Residence also has several rooms with cosy twin beds: an ideal base if you're exploring the city with a friend, your sister or mother and don't necessarily want to share a bed. The Artist Suite is the largest room with high ceilings, a free-standing bathtub in the room, a cosy seat, and a beautiful boudoir: it's many couples' favourite choice for a romantic weekend getaway. The restaurant and café are spread over several spaces on the ground floor. Here you can enjoy a leisurely breakfast among the art, get some work done at a long communal table, or have dinner in the restaurant. A fun mix of locals and guests gather at the bar for drinks in the evening. This is the UK, where beer is the nation's number one tipple, but they also whip up some great cocktails: their Little Miss Sunshine – with grapefruit, honey and prosecco – is a firm favourite. And if you're up for more art after admiring the works in the hotel, the staff will be happy to share their best Bristol art tips.

FROM
170 euro
A NIGHT

www.artistresidence.co.uk
28 Portland Square
Bristol
<< DESIGN STAYS >>

ARTIST RESIDENCE

COUNTRYSIDE

Cowley Manor Experimental

Cotswolds, United Kingdom

92

BEST ROOM:
The Swan Lake suite with a terrace and panoramic views.

NEARBY:
Bibury is one of the most beautiful British villages, just a 20-minute drive away.

TAKE HOME:
The scented candle made especially for the hotel.

SUSTAINABLE EFFORTS:
All the antique cabinets have been preserved, but their doors underwent an upgrade.

DON'T MISS:
The curated audio tour of the gardens, available at the reception.

The English Cotswolds are always beautiful, and September just might be the best time of the year to visit: while the trees are still green after a rainy summer, their tips are already yellow, a sign that autumn is slowly encroaching. One of them has a special story: it is said that Lewis Carroll was so inspired when he sat under this tree in 1890 – gazing at the rabbits, the gardens, and the rolling hills that unfolded before him – that this planted the seed for his world-famous book *Alice in Wonderland*. Cowley Manor Experimental's history is much older, spanning centuries. The stately manor house is listed, as are the Italianate gardens, whose heritage value is deemed even higher. Guests are enticed to take a walk along various lakes on the estate, where you can even have a picnic in tents and where they have an outdoor cinema in summer. Although Cowley Manor has been a hotel since 1999, with a popular spa with an indoor and outdoor pool, it was acquired by the French Experimental Group. The group opened its first cocktail bar in 2007 and now manages bars and hotels in fashionable locations across Europe, from London to Paris, Ibiza to Biarritz. They always work with designer Dorothée Meilichzon, who eschews the usual (Scandinavian) interior design brands, preferring to scour the market for quirky furniture instead. She creates custom-made sinks and baths, and isn't afraid to add a humorous twist to all her design projects. Textile and print lovers won't know where to look first, from the wallpaper, a yellow/beige rug with an organic shape in the reception and of course the headboards of the beds, the designer's signature touch. Everything is equally wonderful. For the interior, Meilichzon was inspired by the property's history, taking a page from Lewis Carroll's book, *Alice in Wonderland*. For example, you can spot a chess board in the games room, rabbit ears in the rug, and the odd secret door. The 33 bedrooms are in the main house and former stables. By Parisian standards, the smallest room would be called a suite, with the doors of the largest suites opening onto the terrace and magnificent views. The restaurant's authentic wooden walls were white before the refurbishment by Experimental. Weeks of painstaking sanding were required before the venue started revealing a glimpse of its former glory. Chef Jackson Boxer creates dishes with local Gloucestershire ingredients and a distinctive French twist. After dinner, pop into the cocktail bar to discover your new favourite drink.

FROM **335** euro A NIGHT

www.cowleymanorexperimental.com

Cowley *Cheltenham*

COWLEY MANOR EXPERIMENTAL

(CITY)

Redchurch Townhouse

London, United Kingdom

98

London's nicest street by far is Redchurch Street in Shoreditch. Here, you can shop at independent boutiques like Labour and Wait, or Earl of East, and eat at nice places like Jolene Bakery, BAO Noodle Shop and Boundary. Established names like Aesop, APC and Toast are also a good idea if you're looking for some retail therapy. The rooms at Redchurch Townhouse are on Redchurch Street, above Cecconi's, but the hotel's official entrance is a little trickier to find. The unassuming door is on a quiet parallel street; once inside, you won't know where to look first. The check-in desk stands out with its white tiles and terrazzo countertop, a striking artwork is the finishing touch in the comfortable seating area, and the slightly dark corridor to the lifts is also lined with art. When the hotel opened, Sara Maple's work *Bloody Neons* was a real Instagram hit. Although Redchurch Townhouse belongs to the Soho House Group, it is a bit of an outlier. Don't expect a massive building with a club, pool, spa, cinema, and multiple restaurants because sleep comes first here. And Italian food at Cecconi's, but that's about it. The hotel has 37 rooms, which are all different. But whether you book the Tiny or the Large, you'll feel comfortable the minute you walk in thanks to the soft colour palette, the high-quality materials, the art, the radio that's playing when you enter the room and the skincare products they provide.

Because there is so much to explore in the area, you don't necessarily need to have a whole living room to yourself. The Large room is worth mentioning, nonetheless, because it is such a luxury to feel what it's like to have a studio of your own in the heart of Shoreditch. The hours pass by very quickly when you have such a view of the street. Sitting on the sofa and starting a new book, or getting out of the bath and bundling up in the hotel's soft bathrobe. You'll obviously want to bag a table at Lyle's around the corner, but should there be none available, Cecconi's is the place to go for Italian cuisine. A pizza, truffle pasta or other delicious food: they have it all and more, and in the morning, breakfast is also served here on Dutch Boerenbont crockery while Shoreditch awakens. Too bad you have to check out before 11 am.

DESIGN STAYS

BEST ROOM:
The Large Room is a suite offering the ultimate in luxury in Shoreditch.

NEARBY:
Redchurch Street is lined with lots of great shops and restaurants. One advantage of spending the night here is that you can be the first in line at Jolene Bakery.

TAKE HOME:
The bathrobe so you can still feel like you're staying at a hotel after returning home.

www.sohohouse.com
25 – 27 Whitby Street London

FROM 250 euro A NIGHT

REDCHURCH TOWNHOUSE

(COUNTRYSIDE)

ROSSO

Altusried, Germany

Running a successful tech company in Hamburg and then shifting your focus to managing a holiday farm in rural southern Germany may seem game-changing, but owner Christian Müller loves his new life. Instead of staring at a screen, he now gets to enjoy vast vistas, a campfire under the stars, and welcoming guests who seek some peace and quiet, albeit for just for a week. Together with Lisa Rühwald, he transformed this farm based on the Japanese philosophy of Wabi Sabi: cherish all that is authentic by acknowledging the principle that nothing lasts, nothing is ever finished, and nothing is perfect. He applied this in the garden surrounding the former farmhouse and the three spacious apartments and yoga room on the ground floor. The couple reused certain materials, found furniture in all kinds of places, and let themselves be surprised by what grows and flowers on the land. But, above all, ROSSO comes alive thanks to all the guests who come to stay there, whether they are a couple, a family with children, a family that wants to rent out the whole farm or the guests of a winter yoga retreat organised by She She Retreats. There are three apartments in the former barn, all with private balconies, lovely bed linens, a kitchen, and a free-standing bathtub.

They all feel welcoming, thanks to art on the wall, a game in the cupboard, and a calendar from the Moon Sisters to look up the moon phase of the day. At ROSSO, you can revel in the beauty of the seasons. In winter, you can go skiing (there are slopes nearby that are especially fun for children and if you drive a little further there's a more challenging ski area), and in summer, you can spend hours in the lush garden, lying on one of the loungers with a good book, or swimming in the natural pool. The sun terrace with its panoramic views is the ultimate spot to enjoy a local German beer and the sunset, after which you head to the rear of the house for a campfire under the stars. There are beehives for fresh honey, you can hear cows and see deer in the distance, and your dog is also welcome. And should you want to leave ROSSO for a few hours, you can go on a hike nearby, forage for truffles or mushrooms, and sample the local cheese.

BEST ROOM:
La Grande overlooking Germany's highest mountain, the Zugspitze.

NEARBY:
Take your kids skiing in the Adelegg Mountains (about half an hour away).

TAKE HOME:
Vino Rosso, their house wine, the fruit of their partnership with a young woman winemaker from Lake Constance.

SUSTAINABLE EFFORTS:
They make compost from guests' organic waste and then use it in the garden to grow fruit and vegetables.

FROM 220 euro A NIGHT

Oberhub 3
Altusried
www.dasrosso.com

DESIGN STAYS

Château Royal
Berlin, Germany

110

When you check in at Château Royal, you not only get a key card to the room but also a map of all the artworks hanging on the hotel's walls. The 18th-century building, stripped of its original details during the GDR era, has been lovingly restored to its former glory by David Chipperfield Architects, who are also known for, among many other acclaimed projects, their renovation of the Neue Nationalgalerie. After the architectural master plan was finalised, interior designer Irina Kromayer and art curator Kirsten Landwehr came on board, giving the hotel, bar and restaurant a new look and feel that does justice to the building's stature, and will also put a smile on your face now and then. Take the collection of cheerful-looking images in the stairwell by artist Lena Schramm, for example, which turn out to be inspired by XTC pills. The entrepreneurs behind the hotel already had experience with restaurants, having previously opened Le Petit Royal, Kin Dee and Grill Royal, before opening their first hotel on a side street of Unter den Linden, lined with embassies. Château Royal also has a restaurant on the ground floor, with classic and Mediterranean fare on the menu. One of the bestsellers is the Château Royal Burger, a vegan version of this classic dish. The wine list is also excellent, with up to 250 different wines. Some are from Germany, most from Europe, including some excellent champagnes and Burgundies. In summer, you can head to the rooftop terrace, where you can order a quick pizza for ten euros with views of the Reichstag on one side and the Fernsehturm on the other. The rooms are all different, mainly in size, art and colour scheme. The medium room has two baby blue round armchairs, a spacious bathroom, and a TV hidden in an ottoman at the end of the bed. The Tower Suite has a turret with a rocking chair and a freestanding bath. If you do decide to leave the hotel, you can walk to the Brandenburger Tor and the large Tiergarten city park behind it in just seven minutes.

DESIGN STAYS

BEST ROOM:
The suites are spacious and have a freestanding bath.

NEARBY:
Bonanza Coffee bar on Jägerstraße next to Galeries Lafayette.

TAKE HOME:
The hotel almost can't keep up with demand for its Château Royal caps.

SUSTAINABLE EFFORTS:
Instead of polluting Nespresso cups in the room, there's a filter coffee drip bag that Bonanza Coffee made especially for the hotel.

Neustädtische Kirchstraße 3
Berlin
www.chateauroyalberlin.com

FROM 195 euro A NIGHT

CHÂTEAU ROYAL

Wilmina

Berlin, Germany

116

Hidden in the heart of Charlottenburg is Wilmina, a hotel in a former women's prison. A place with a rich history where resistance heroines were imprisoned during World War II and where, after the prison's closure in 1985, *The Reader*, starring Kate Winslet and Ralph Fiennes, was filmed. The idea of spending the night there, with bars still on the windows, may not appeal to everyone – until you find out that Grüntuch Ernst Architects was in charge of the renovation, which took several years. Previous projects of this renowned Berlin-based architectural firm include the former Jewish Girls' School and the Hackesches Quartier in Mitte. Reconstructing a prison is far from easy. How do you turn an anti-social place into a social place while retaining the bars, prison doors with tiny shutters, and ultra-thick doors and walls? But they pulled it off, as today it's safe to call this a luxury hotel, while the property's history has been admirably preserved. Check-in takes place at the reception on busy Kantstrasse, after which you walk through the courtyard of the former courthouse and arrive at a large gate. When these doors open, you enter a peaceful, verdant oasis with greenery everywhere you look, birdsong in the background and a view of Lovis, Wilmina's restaurant. The path takes you to the hotel entrance, from where you can explore different areas: the breakfast room, a communal living room, the gym, and the outdoor courtyard where prisoners used to

go for a walk and where they have now installed some tables for sunny days. The lift takes you upstairs to a cell block with a corridor where the original cell doors conceal luxurious rooms. If you want more space, floor-to-ceiling windows and a bath, then the Penthouse Suite is the way to go. Another luxury the inmates did not have is access to the rooftop terrace and a swimming pool and sauna. You can dine at Lovis, where chef Sophia Rudolph, who formerly worked at Panama restaurant, promotes German gastronomy. And if you want to explore more of the surrounding area, there are always the restaurants and bars around Savignyplatz, or you can immerse yourself in nature. Forest Grunewald is just a 20-minute trip by bike.

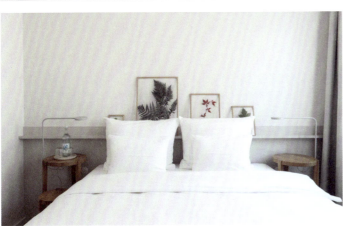

FROM
160 euro
A NIGHT

Kantstrasse 79
Berlin
www.wilmina.com

BEST ROOM:
The Classic rooms are where the building's history is most tangible.

NEARBY:
Pars Restaurant is all about fine dining and chocolates.

TAKE HOME:
The Frama hand soap is a lovely memento of your stay.

SUSTAINABLE EFFORTS:
In 2022, they received the German Sustainability Award for Architecture for the many sustainable methods that were applied to transform a monumental prison into a hotel.

DESIGN STAYS

(CITY)

Warszauer

Kraków, Poland

Jewellery designer Marta Gajewska always wanted to open a breakfast bar. While searching for a location in Kraków, she found a completely run-down beer pub in the city's Jewish quarter, Kazimierz. She immediately realised the place had potential, abandoning her original plan and working vertically to create ten luxury hotel rooms in the building. The breakfast room is on the ground floor and is the Warszauer's beating heart. It took ten years for the permits to be finalised and the neighbours to give the green light, but the hotel's doors finally opened in 2022. These days, you'll find plenty of independent boutique hotels in most

cities, but in Kraków, where the hotel market is dominated by hotel chains, a small-scale hotel with a few uniquely decorated rooms is still quite exceptional. The owner enlisted the help of INDO Architekci for the structure and the striking façade, designing the interiors of the rooms and the common areas herself. She prioritised the high quality of the materials, such as Italian marble in the bathrooms, but also made sure that there was at least one design piece in every room, including a Zig Zag chair by Rietveld in some rooms but also Frama bedside tables, armchairs by &Tradition, and chairs by Hay and Bruno Rey. Many items were custom-made for the hotel, such as the wooden furniture with the built-in minibar. In one of the rooms, this thick wood was also used for the doors that separate the seating area from the bedroom. The Polish collaborations are particularly exciting. The art in the hotel was created by Tomek Opaliński, the sculptures by Jan Krzysztof, and the ceramics by Klo Ceramics. The breakfast room is perhaps the most beautiful place in the hotel where the owner has clearly poured all her love for the first meal of the day into a photoworthy décor. Dishes like omelettes, pancakes, and oatmeal make for an excellent start of the day and are served at a communal table, which is a great conversation starter. By 9 am, you should already have scored some fun tips for your city visit. In the evening, you can rent out the restaurant and renowned Polish/Jewish chef Adam Gessler will prepare a four-course meal for you while telling you more about the neighbourhood's history. You will even be treated to live music. Of course there are lots of other restaurants in the Kazimierz district worth discovering.

BEST ROOM:
The two-storey Penthouse has a large window, while the Apartment Deluxe is slightly more compact and also very bright.

NEARBY:
Book a table at Youmiko Sushi or sit at the bar and watch the chefs prepare their sushi.

SUSTAINABLE EFFORTS:
They work with sustainable materials, use local products throughout the hotel, and have an efficient energy system for heating/cooling the rooms.

www.warszauer.com
Warszauera 10, Kraków
FROM 97 euro A NIGHT

(COUNTRYSIDE)

Experimental Chalet

Verbier, Switzerland

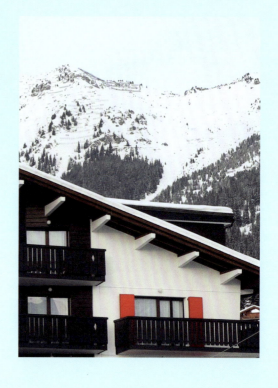

128

If you love skiing and design, options can feel limited, unless you don't mind sleeping in a wood-clad chalet-style hotel room. Not exactly the pinnacle of sophistication, but Parisian Experimental Group has now upped the ante, hiring an Italian designer for their first mountain hotel. Fabrizio Casiraghi has earned a reputation for bold combinations with his projects ranging from Parisian residences and restaurants in St Tropez. He makes imaginative use of light and colour and effortlessly pairs antique furniture with subtle twists. For Experimental Chalet, he drew inspiration from his childhood in Tyrol, combined with influences from the Bauhaus period and the 1950s. The lamps

in the restaurant and on the bedside table have a Bauhaus look and feel, while the Edelweiss print on the rug in the room is a nod to his childhood. The hotel's restaurant and bar in the heart of Verbier, one of Europe's most exclusive ski resorts, welcome guests and locals alike. It's the kind of place where you may bump into British Royals, as they also own homes here, but ultimately, all everyone really cares about are the 410 kilometres of pistes in the Les 4 Vallées area. With its unbeatable views, the 3,300-metre descent from Mont-Fort is for more advanced skiers. A shuttle bus will take you from the hotel to the ski lift, where your adventure begins. When it's time for après-ski, you can head to one of the surrounding bars. The Experimental Group's cocktails are legendary, however, so Experimental Chalet also has a stylish in-house cocktail bar, and there's also the well-known nightclub the Farm Club downstairs if you're ready to take to the dance floor. The restaurant is overseen by chef Gregory Marchand of Frenchie in Paris. The menu includes a vegetarian cauliflower soup as well as Cavatelli, a vegetarian pasta dish made with vin jaune, Swiss cheese and mushrooms. The Frenchie Bannofee, their signature dessert with banana and caramel, is to die for. Instead of wood-clad rooms, the walls have been painted in a bright colour palette of white, green and red, with an old-fashioned print of mountains above the bed. The suites have panoramic mountain views and a jacuzzi on the terrace. You'll also find one on the spa terrace, where guests can treat their muscles to a well-deserved massage after a day on the slopes.

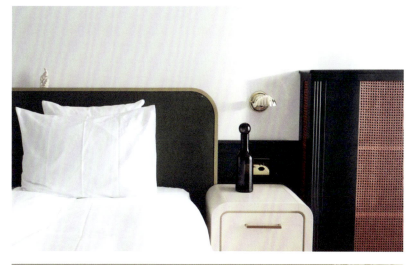

BEST ROOM:
The Panorama Suite has insane views over three terraces and a fireplace in the living room.

NEARBY:
Restaurants Dahu and Chez Dany, both on the slopes.

TAKE HOME:
The Experimental Chalet scented candle.

SUSTAINABLE EFFORTS:
The hotel has partnered with Circle Supply Co, a company specialising in the rental of outdoor and skiwear through hotels. It's a way to inspire people to buy less and they'll have your ski clothes ready for you when you arrive at the hotel.

Route de Verbier, Station 55
Verbier
www.experimentalchalet.com

FROM 330 euro A NIGHT

131 EXPERIMENTAL CHALET

[COUNTRYSIDE]

Le Barn

Bonnelles, France

134

Just a 45-minute drive from Paris in the Haute Vallée de Chevreuse natural park, and next to La Cense, the famous stud farm of its co-founder William Kriegel, is Le Barn, a unique estate where both adults and children find time to unwind. There somehow always seem to be more minutes in an hour in a place like this: time just seems to pass by more slowly because you automatically go along with the rhythm of nature. Horses welcome you upon arrival, and Sailor the dog bounds over, tail wagging, as you make your way to the check-in desk with your suitcases. The main building has several comfortable sofas and armchairs, a cupboard full of (French) books, and lots of art on the walls. La Serre, the hotel's restaurant serves refined dishes made with seasonal produce from their own vegetable garden or sourced from nearby farmers. There is a large terrace out front where you can sit comfortably all year round. And in case rain showers come rolling in, the hotel has thoughtfully provided raincoats at the entrance. Children love to run around on the courtyard while their imagination is stimulated by the vast estate with swings, tree houses, a lake, and a chest filled with creative dress-up costumes. On bad weather days, they keep you entertained with a nice movie in the cinema. Adults are also inspired by the surrounding nature. Many lovely hiking and mountain biking trails are nearby, and there's an 18-hole golf course a little further

afield. The La Cense method of William Kriegel, one of Le Barn's founders, is famous worldwide for teaching people to interact with horses in a holistic way. If you're a rider, whether a beginner or more experienced, you have definitely come to the right place. Horse lovers can combine nature sightseeing with a nice ride. But wait a minute: instead of filling your weekend schedule with activities, you'll find that at Le Barn, it's better to go with the flow. Sleep in and wake up to a magical lake view, read a book, and, who knows, maybe even book a relaxing massage in the spa. Le Barn's interior invites you to live life in the slow(er) lane: Parisian design studio Be-Pôles (which also designed the interior of Le Pigalle in Paris and Les Roches Rouges on the Côte d'Azur) has succeeded in creating a cosy atmosphere, without too many frills. The bedroom has a natural colour scheme, with high-quality materials like the thick Barbour curtains and the comfy Zip Dee camping chairs.

BEST ROOM:
752 if you want to see the sun rise over the forest in the morning.

NEARBY:
Haras de La Cense for the ultimate horse whisperer experience.

TAKE HOME:
The delicately scented shower gel, specially formulated by Saint-Lazare for Le Barn.

SUSTAINABLE EFFORTS:
Le Barn has a (swimming) pond instead of a pool.

DON'T MISS:
Sign up for an analogue photography contact print workshop in their *chambre noire* (dark room).

www.lebarnhotel.com
Moulin de Brétigny
Bonnelles
DESIGN STAYS

FROM
235 euro
A NIGHT

(COUNTRYSIDE)

Le Moulin

Lourmarin, France

140

BEST ROOM:
The Deluxe Family Room is just right for two adults and two children under 12.

NEARBY:
Apart from Lourmarin and Provence's lavender fields, you should also consider visiting Château la Coste. The wine estate, with a restaurant designed by Japanese architect Tadao Ando, has an impressive collection of outdoor sculptures and architecture by Louise Bourgeois, Alexander Calder and others (it's a short half-hour drive from the hotel).

TAKE HOME:
Homemade jam from Les Commissions.

DON'T MISS:
The Pétanque Apéro.

Lourmarin is one of the most picturesque villages in Provence. Its traditional Provençal houses are covered in ivy, you may spot the odd old Renault 4 parked on the street, and the terraces are full of people enjoying an afternoon glass of pastis – wearing a fedora of course, a true holiday wardrobe staple. In the village centre, Le Moulin (a former mill) has been transformed into a hotel. The kind of hotel where you only have to open the shutters to see the picturesque, almost film-like setting in front of you, complete with the sound of church bells in the background. Certain destinations are inextricably linked with specific scents, and here at Le Moulin, they chose to stock the bathrooms with the Philosykos scent by French (home) perfume brand Diptyque. The bathroom is lined with terracotta tiles and has a curtain to hide your towels. Authentic, but with a modern twist. The hotel's interior was designed by JAUNE Architects, the two Parisian women who also created the interior of Baja Club Hotel in Mexico and one of the Liberté bakeries in Paris. They combined a warm colour palette with a sisal floor, wall coverings and lots of ceramics and art. The restaurant is on the ground floor, as is the more casual lounge by the lobby, where you can grab a drink or flip open your laptop. The menu features dishes inspired by the seasons, as chef Thibaud Chadebec sources all the fresh ingredients for his Provençal recipes from nearby farms and local food makers. Most dishes are either oven-grilled or cooked on the barbecue. While the restaurant is aesthetically pleasing, dining in the sheltered garden with romantic lighting is the way to go if you're looking for that authentic south-of-France-vibe. The other terrace, which gives out onto one of the village streets, is no different. It's a great place to watch local residents and tourists pass by as you sip your cup of morning coffee. Next door is Les Commissions, a deli with all kinds of tasty local produce which you can take back home with you. Le Moulin is owned by the small Beaumier hotel group, whose portfolio also includes Les Roches Rouges on the French Riviera and Le Val Thorens in the French Alps. Besides offering their guests a fabulous experience, they also want to help them discover some of France's most beautiful regions from a different angle. At Le Moulin they propose really unique experiences; you can book a bike tour with a picnic for example, or take an outdoor yoga class.

LE MOULIN

145   LE MOULIN

(CITY)

Tuba

Marseille, France

146

FROM
230 euro
A NIGHT

2 boulevard
Alexandre Delabre,
village des Goudes
Marseille
www.tuba-club.com

BEST ROOM:
The Villa Suite is the largest, but room 3 is the only room with a private terrace.

NEARBY:
Discover the Calanques Natural Park and its beautiful azure waters.

TAKE HOME:
The handmade ashtrays with the Tuba or Le Bikini's logo.

SUSTAINABLE EFFORTS:
Help keep the sea clean by taking a bin bag with you when you go for a dip. If you return with at least five plastics, the hotel will offer you a drink on the house.

Tuba is in Marseille, even though some locals describe it as being at "the end of the world": from the old port of Marseille, you drive about 30 minutes to get to a small fishing village called Les Goudes, close to the picture-perfect Calanques natural park. The entrance to Tuba is hard to find: at the street level there's nothing more than a door, which opens into a small stairwell where the artist Emmanuelle Luciani of Southway Studio created the wall and ceiling paintings. As you make your way downstairs you realise that this was once a diving school, as a long, narrow corridor with old flippers and pictures of the olden days leads to the lobby. Prepare for your jaw to drop, because the view of the sea and the surrounding mountain ranges is breathtakingly beautiful. Throw in some salty sea air and a fresh breeze, and you can imagine what it must have been like in the days when divers slipped on their suits, walked down the steps, and leapt into the water from the rocks. Today, however, a sunny terrace and restaurant with a 60s vibe await. Yellow and white loungers, white parasols, and old director's chairs beckon, encouraging you to sunbathe, read, and enjoy good food. The restaurant's menu reads like a best of the region. They cook with the catch of the day, combining this with other Mediterranean influences. A Greek salad, Sicilian sweets, it's all there, but the emphasis is clearly on seafood. As you enter, you'll be asked what you want to drink. At Le Bikini's, a bar in an old ship's hull, they whip up cocktails all day, serving them with some light fare. The perfect option if you're looking to spend the day on your sun lounger enjoying the surroundings. The hotel opened in the summer of 2020 and is a popular haunt with tourists as well as with the local creative crowd. It was designed by Marion Mailaender, who has her roots in Marseille but has since established her architecture firm in Paris, although she still travels back and forth regularly. She used the property's

history as inspiration for the interior, pairing local materials with vintage furniture. There are three villas and five rooms. The 15-m² rooms all have views of the sea and rocks surrounding the hotel, with snorkels and flippers waiting for you in the closet. The villas are much more spacious (from 18 m² to 55 m²) and have large windows with the best views and additional seating. Who would think the end of the world looks a lot like paradise?

CITY

Hotel HOY

Paris, France

HOY stands for House of Yoga and is a hotel designed with the philosophy of yoga in mind. Owner Charlotte Gomez de Orozco observed the rise of well-being retreats in inspiring places in nature and concluded that busy thirty-somethings and forty-somethings needed a city equivalent. Not necessarily with a full-time seven-day programme, but offering guests the facilities to unwind and focus after visiting busy Paris, whether during a yoga class or by lighting incense in their room. She partnered up with YUJ Yoga, a Parisian yoga school with six branches in the city. They're popular because of the infrared lights they use during classes; the heat increases flexibility, cleanses the body and helps to drain toxins. YUJ offers different types of classes, from a deepening Yin Detox to an energetic Flow Mix. Once a month, they also organise a Sound Bath for deep relaxation. HOY also means 'today' in Spanish, a reference to their motto to take care of your today for a better future. This is also the first thing you notice as a guest when you enter, breathe in, and the scent of Palo Santo helps you unwind. The hotel staff's friendly and, above all, calm demeanour only makes you feel even more at ease. Taking action today for a better future also takes place on a deeper sustainable level. Here, food scraps are recycled, they promote short food circuits by working with local food makers and, as a guest, you are encouraged to take the stairs instead of the lift. The bedrooms are fitted with an air freshening system, you get a carafe of tap water in which charcoal is used as a water filter, and the bathroom products are of course organic and French-made. At MESA, the hotel's restaurant, the menu is 100% plant-based and inspired by the Latin American roots of the owners. In the evening, you can order their seasonal Experience Menu, which is both gluten-free and vegan and features for example wild asparagus as a starter or tamale as a main course. The dish everyone keeps coming back for are the purple corn pancakes: a stack of pancakes with jam, vanilla yoghurt and toasted almond butter. It's also great for sharing. You'll find there's actually no need for you to leave the hotel, but this would be a shame, as bustling Pigalle is right there, begging to be discovered.

BEST ROOM:
The light in the Suite is lovely, and the bed has a blissfully soft duvet cover.

NEARBY:
The hotel is in the heart of Pigalle, home to culinary hotspots like Bouillon Pigalle, Frenchie, and Rose Bakery.

TAKE HOME:
A hoodie from HOY and some Palo Santo to imbue your suitcase with its lovely scent.

DON'T MISS:
The hotel's workshops like KAP Kundalini yoga and ceramics workshops.

CITY

Le Pigalle

Paris, France

Pigalle was formerly known as Paris's red-light district. Even though hip establishments like Frenchie, Soho House and Pink Mamma now call this neighbourhood home, you still find remnants of sex, drugs, and rock & roll in its streets. The Moulin Rouge still captures visitors' imagination today, as do the neon lights on the streets and the fact that hospitality venues like to accentuate this forbidden, libertine history by calling their bar Dirty Dick, for example. Or in the case of Le Pigalle, by having a stripper's pole in the lobby, complete with red plush and mirrors. Le Pigalle was a real pioneer, opening their neighbourhood hotel back in 2015. While guests were welcomed with open arms, the hotel's primary target audience was the locals, who like to drink cocktails in the lobby until late, after which they heed the DJ's call and dance the night away on the very intimate dance floor. Musicians, artists, and other creative minds, they're all here. There may not be a lot of space, but the ambience is always great. While this is partly the merit of the guests and colourful staff, the interior also adds an unmistakable *je ne sais quoi*, providing the ideal backdrop. Eye-catchers include a De Sede sofa, a Soriana lounge chair by Cassina, and other mid-century-inspired furniture and accessories. All of this is the work of architects Charlotte de Tonnac and Hugo Sauzay of Festen Architecture, who also have hotel Les Roches Rouges in the south of France and Rochechouart (also in Pigalle) to their names. Here they paired design classics with illustrations by local artist Artus de Lavilléon, vases with bunches of flowers, and bistro chairs, creating a lively atmosphere. There's no need to worry about where to sit, as the paintings aren't perfectly aligned either. Le Pigalle is in a typical French building, so don't expect long hotel corridors with uniform rooms on either side. All the rooms are unique. What's more, they feel like home: a record player in the room, artwork above the bed, and some great magazines on the table. Open the windows to gaze out onto the neighbourhood and feel like a true *Parisienne* or *Parisien*. To start your day with a croissant and a cup of coffee, head to Café Pigalle, where you can watch the residents of Pigalle file by on the typical French terrace out front.

BEST ROOM:
Room type Pigalle 22 has a freestanding bathtub overlooking the patio. The photos were taken in room type 21, for vinyl lovers.

NEARBY:
Besides Café Pigalle, you can also check out the famous Pigalle basketball court around the corner.

TAKE HOME:
Matches: the unique design was created by local tattoo artist Jean-Andre of Bonjour Tattoo Club.

SUSTAINABLE EFFORTS:
Le Pigalle partners with local artists, uses recycled soap, and donates money to improve the sanitation of families in need.

161   LE PIGALLE

COUNTRYSIDE

D'une île

Rémalard, France

164

BEST ROOM:

The Grande Suite is the most romantic option, with a free-standing bathtub you'll never want to get out of.

NEARBY:

Head to Studio 7 Avril in Bellême for furniture, clothes and much more, and to Chez Nous Campagne for lunch and brocante.

TAKE HOME:

The hotel's limited edition beer. Every year, they launch a new one with Deck & Donohue, using the herbs or fruit growing at D'une île. Previous creations include a blackberry beer, a blackcurrant beer, and an elderflower beer.

SUSTAINABLE EFFORTS:

They use only regionally sourced ingredients. So no olive oil as there are no olive groves in Normandy. The fish on the menu is locally sourced, and the vegetables are harvested from the garden.

A Dutch couple lovingly created this paradise near Le Perche natural park in green and hilly Normandy, just over a two-hour drive from Paris. They set about transforming the former country house into a number of basic but stylishly decorated rooms and apartments, naming it D'une île. In the summer of 2018, chef Bertrand Grébaut and his business partner Théophile Pourriat of Septime in Paris, among others, acquired the house and the surrounding land, and brought a new restaurant and wine bar to Normandy. Their restaurants in Paris, including Septime, which was awarded a (green) Michelin star, were already sourcing ingredients from Normandy where possible. But now, they are assured of a constant supply as they have established their own vegetable garden on the estate. The menu at D'une île also relies heavily on seasonal produce from local farms, markets and of course harvested from its own garden. After checking into the rustic restaurant where guests are welcomed with a homemade lemonade and fresh madeleines, you can't help but notice the busy kitchen. There's a lot of cutting,

cooking, and fermenting going on, and the blissful smell emanating from the kitchen makes you salivate at the thought of the three-course dinner that will be served in the evening. Guests eat indoors or outdoors (this is Normandy, after all, and summer showers are unpredictable). The bedrooms and apartments are decorated with finds from the many nearby flea markets, punctuated with the odd Dutch memento, such as a poster of Toneelgroep Oostpool. There are 25-m^2 rooms, but you can also book the 110-m^2 Super Suite for up to six people. This indicates that D'une île is also popular with families with children. They can let their imagination run wild on the estate, as they climb on tree stumps, play on the swings, or follow the black cat. Don't bother bringing an iPad as the reach is almost non-existent. Instead, relax in the Artifort F587 armchair with a book while the fireplace crackles softly in the background, or take a dip in the pool on warmer days. There is plenty to do nearby if you love a good hike, but the surrounding picturesque villages, such as Bellême, are also worth visiting. Looking to score some flea market gems? Enquire with the staff about the custom route that will lead you to all the best addresses.

Casa Bonay

Barcelona,
Spain

170

Even though she's the co-founder, Inés Miró-Sans always insists that the success of ever popular Casa Bonay in Barcelona is, and forever will be, largely the merit of a collaboration with local artists, designers, and brands. Originally from Barcelona, Miró-Sans has travelled the world. In Brooklyn, she discovered Post Company, the design studio she eventually partnered up with for the architecture of the huge former textile factory where the hotel is housed. Post Company's work is possibly the only non-Spanish feature here, as everything else in

the hotel has a story revolving around Spanish makers. Marc Morro is an independent, Barcelona-based furniture maker who, among other things, created the wooden pieces in the rooms, as well as the entire reception desk and the tables on the roof terrace. All the lighting in the hotel comes from Santa & Cole, while the plaids on the bed are by Teixidors. Casa Bonay is located along the busy Gran Via in the central Eixample district. If you want, you can spend the day at the hotel without ever feeling bored. You could start by buying the latest copy of *Apartamento* magazine from their bookshop in the lobby. Then order a cup of coffee from local specialty coffee brand Nomad Coffee and already read some articles in your magazine in the TosTao coffee bar or in Libertine, the spacious lobby where Marc Morro revamped Miguel Milá's unique chairs. Libertine is the hotel's beating heart, where you can flip open your laptop to get some work done, and where everyone takes to the dance floor after hours while the DJ spins some tunes. If you prefer to sit outside, take the lift to the rooftop terrace called Chiringuito, which means 'small bar' in Spanish. As its name suggests, this rooftop beach club serves wine, cocktails and tapas. If you're a hotel guest and you prefer some peace and quiet, you can head to the guest-only area where you can get some reading done on a lounger or even take a yoga class. Hungry? Then you'll be happy to know they have a sustainable restaurant called Bodega Bonay on the ground floor, with a menu of mostly Mediterranean dishes and (natural) wine. And if you want to sleep peacefully at night, retreat to the modern version of a typical Catalan bedroom with high ceilings and a unique mosaic floor. *Bona nit.*

CASA BONAY

FROM 180 euro A NIGHT
www.casabonay.com
Gran Via de les Corts Catalanes 700 Barcelona

BEST ROOM:
The Courtyard Large Terrace. This room has a spacious balcony with an outdoor shower. Perfect for cooling off after a hot day in the city.

NEARBY:
Funky Bakers Eatery serves blissful lunch fare and pastries while Lot Roasters does the most amazing things with chocolate.

TAKE HOME:
Something from The Souvenir Store where they sell ceramics, T-shirts, jewellery, and cosmetics from local entrepreneurs.

SUSTAINABLE EFFORTS:
In addition to their comprehensive sustainable action plan, Casa Bonay aims to help one homeless person get off the streets every year, for which it has partnered with two charities, called Arrels and Mambre.

DESIGN STAYS

(COUNTRYSIDE)

Little Beach House

Garraf, Spain

176

They call it Little Beach House Barcelona because it is only a thirty-minute drive from its sister hotel, Soho House, in the heart of Barcelona. But here you are in Garraf, a small seaside resort to the south of the city. Soho House is a UK-based hotel group where creative and entrepreneurial members can spend the night, but mostly value the opportunity to build a network on the club floors and during the events Soho House organises in their venues worldwide. What started with a hotel in London has since expanded to include a portfolio of houses around the world, from Mumbai to Malibu and from Berlin to Bangkok. As its name suggests, Little Beach House is one of the smaller houses, but it also has one of the most amazing views from the lobby. Staying focussed during check-in is difficult as your eyes cannot help but drift to the large square window to your right, which opens onto the sea. Because here, the Mediterranean really is on your doorstep. It also means that when you stand on the balcony of your room five minutes later and take a deep breath, you smell the sea, hear the waves crashing on the beach, with the horizon before you. Suddenly your everyday life seems far away. Soho House employs a design team that finds unique (vintage) furniture for all the houses and a curator who aims to get the work of as many (young) artists on the walls as possible. For example, the tapestries at Little Beach House Garraf were created by Maryanne Moodie. Nowadays, every hotel claims to want to make guests feel at home, but Nick Jones, Soho House's founder, was the first to voice this ambition when he opened the first house back in 1995. As a guest, you'll find that you can pack lightly because the bathrooms are stocked with the most amazing shampoos and shower gels, and you can also use their skincare line. The pillow menu has seven different options to choose from to avoid tossing and turning. The ground floor restaurant opens out to the sea, and your day off starts on one of the sun loungers out front. An added bonus are the daily events they organise, and as there is a major observatory nearby, stargazing can be one of them. A fun way to learn something new and meet new people.

BEST ROOM:
The Terrace rooms and Beach Studio have a freestanding bathtub on the terrace. Not a bad sight to wake up to.

NEARBY:
La Caseta is their version of a beach club inspired by the authentic green and white beach houses of Garraf.

TAKE HOME:
The 24/7 Treatment from the Soho Skin product line is both a blissful mask and a nourishing night cream.

SUSTAINABLE EFFORTS:
They organise a beach clean-up in which Garraf locals, Little Beach House staff, and Soho House members can participate. The festive finale is a lunch together.

FROM 300 euro A NIGHT

www.sohohouse.com
Carrer Mirador del Port 1
Garraf

LITTLE BEACH HOUSE

(COUNTRYSIDE)

Los Enamorados

Ibiza, Spain

BEST ROOM:

Room two because of B&B Italia's Big Mama chair. It's also the only room with a hammock on the balcony.

NEARBY:

Walk to the lighthouse from the hotel. There's a tiny beach that is not that well-known and where you can swim in the nude.

TAKE HOME:

Bring an extra suitcase because the hotel shop is irresistible. Didn't think of bringing one? A sweater from Los Enamorados is a great keepsake.

SUSTAINABLE EFFORTS:

Having the sea instead of a swimming pool reduces water bills tremendously. The garden is planted with succulents and cacti because they need less water, a scarce commodity in Ibiza.

Los enamorados means 'the lovers' in Spanish and if you look closely, you will see the mural of the loving couple and owners Rozemarijn de Witte and Pierre Traversier on the side of what was once a typical Spanish *hostal* in the far north of Ibiza. She's originally from the Netherlands, and he's French. The couple divides their time between Amsterdam, Paris, Ibiza, and wherever their travels take them. If you're into minimalist hotels with just one accessory in the hotel room, don't stop here, because the lady of the house is a keen collector of all things colourful, including many objects with a 70s vibe that put a smile on your face. Take off your shoes, feel the carpet under your feet, and take your time to explore everything. That's how you might find yourself falling in love with a 70-centimetre-high wicker banana or two wooden panels with a nose on which you can store your sunglasses. You might even end up strolling around in a kaftan in no time. And that's just the shop. The hotel is not exclusive to guests, with the shop and restaurant attracting people from all over the island, including on Friday nights when there is dancing to African music. Local chef Alexander van der Hagen serves seasonal dishes on the spacious terrace, with the prawn taco being a firm favourite. The restaurant overlooks the bay of Portinatx and its bobbing boats. You may even spot an evening swimmer while you wait for the sunset. It probably doesn't come as a surprise that colour is everywhere here as well, with an unruly mix of furniture and a covetable selection of table linen and ceramics. It's hard to believe that this nine-bedroom hotel once used to be a fluorescent-lit hostal with a marble floor, although the owners did retain the wooden slatted ceilings in the rooms. The beds are dreamy, with a mosquito net and thick, colourful bedding. There's an Up50 chair by B&B Italia in the corner and a hammock on the bay view terrace. Ibiza can be a bit showy sometimes, and in some parts of the island restaurants tend to up their prices because the customer always pays anyway. But you'll still find plenty of places that stick to fair prices; the hotel owners recommend restaurant Hämbre in Santa Eularia.

187 LOS ENAMORADOS

(COUNTRYSIDE)

Casa de las Flores

Lanzarote, Spain

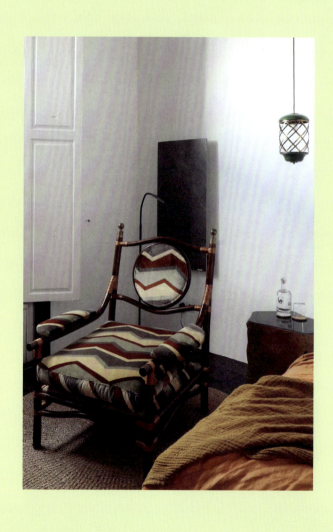

188

Óscar Cubillo spent much of his life working for the world's most luxurious hotel chains. He is used to guests' suitcases being unpacked for them and offering them a pillow menu. His dream was to one day open his own hospitality business, with the same five-star service, but in an intimate setting. He was born on lush green Tenerife but fell in love with the lava island of Lanzarote, where he and stylist and costume designer Gigi de Vidal initially set out to find a place for themselves to live. However, when they walked into this property in the picturesque village of Teguise, they immediately realised that they wanted to share it with others. And so they set to work. The corner building from 1785, with its high ceilings, central patio, and a fairly wide corridor connecting the rooms, needed quite some love before they could welcome the first guests to their bed and breakfast. Layers and layers of paint were stripped from doorposts to reveal the original wood, and the couple started looking for (secondhand) furniture and art. De Vidal used her knowledge of textiles to reupholster an armchair and create wall hangings for above the beds. The bathrooms are spa-worthy: they're spacious and bright and one of the rooms (El Gabinete) even has a large fern hanging in the shower. Casa de las Flores has five spacious rooms. El Balcón, on the top floor, offers a panoramic view from the balcony as well as from the bathroom. El Patio is the largest suite, with a private pool and a picture-perfect striped sofa in the room. Comfortable beds are an important feature at Casa de las Flores, but the ultimate experience here is breakfast. Guests are expected at 9 am at the long communal table in the dining room where the first thing to catch your eye is the table setting – make sure to check out the fork and spoon-shaped handles on the wooden cabinet. After you meet your fellow guests and exchange some island tips, the three-course breakfast is served. The menu rotates daily, so you can try everything if you stay for the week. Everything is homemade, from the yoghurt with fruit to the omelette and muffin for dessert. What better way to start your day?

DESIGN STAYS

BEST ROOM:
El Cuarto is the room featured in the photos, with a large bathroom and a dreamy bed.

NEARBY:
Famous surf spot Famara is just a 15-minute drive, and also actor Omar Sharif's impressive house (Museo Lagomar) is five minutes from Casa de las Flores.

TAKE HOME:
The house fragrance remains a secret success, but guests who stay in the suites are given a bottle to take home to extend their experience.

DON'T MISS:
SECA Studio, Gigi de Vidal's studio, creates clothes for guests to wear during their stay and which you can buy afterwards if you want.

FROM 150 euro A NIGHT

Calle las Flores 1, Teguise
Lanzarote
www.hotelcasadelasflores.es

CASA DE LAS FLORES

CITY

Yours

Valencia,
Spain

194

FROM 150 euro A NIGHT

www.thisisyours.es
Carrer Cuba 19
Valencia

BEST ROOM:
The Apartment has a nice breezy layout.

NEARBY:
Bluebell Coffee for lunch, Fran Café for coffee, and Hikari Yakitori bar for dinner.

TAKE HOME:
The hotel's signature fragrance in candle form.

SUSTAINABLE EFFORTS:
They use refillable personal care products from Marie Stella Maris, clean with cleaning products that can be mixed with water to reduce plastic consumption, and have an à la carte breakfast menu to reduce food waste.

The Dutch owners of Yours, Daphne Kniest and Wouter Kock, had been running a thriving B&B in Valencia for several years before stumbling upon an abandoned laundrette in Ruzafa, one of the city's coolest districts. They thought it had potential for a hotel, and signed the contract just before the pandemic began. While the renovation took longer than expected, it also allowed them to collaborate with local designers. The chairs and tables are by Viccarbe, the lights by Arkoslight, and the ceramics by La Navà. This way, the hotel has some Spanish flair in combination with its Scandi aesthetic. The soft colour palette has a soothing effect in a neighbourhood where people dine on the streets until late and stop for drinks in one of the cosy bars. The reception is disguised as a bar surrounded by several seating areas overlooking the plunge pool on the patio. The owners wanted this space to feel like a living room for guests, and that is precisely what it is. Here you'll easily get to know the staff who are happy to share tips about the city and whip up a blissful breakfast with fresh juice and açai bowls. The pool is an easy place to strike up a chat with other guests. It's not necessarily the place you might want to go for some laps, but if you're looking to rinse off the heat of Valencia, a quick plunge – or a cold (outdoor) shower – will do the trick. But you can also retreat to one of the spacious rooms, of course. The smallest room type is 28 m^2 and has a French balcony, bed, lounge sofa, and bathroom. The Apartment and Penthouse have a kitchen, making them ideal for people who want to spend more time in the city. The Penthouse also has a lovely private terrace. Valencia is the kind of city you should explore by bike, and Yours rents out cool Veloretti bikes that will get you to the beach in about 20 minutes and to the City of Arts and Sciences, an architectural highlight by Valencia-born architect Santiago Calatrava, in just 11 minutes. If you don't feel like biking, you can take a walk in the Ruzafa district, where you will find many unique shops and restaurants.

(COUNTRYSIDE)

São Lourenço do Barrocal

Barrocal, Portugal

198

São Lourenço do Barrocal is situated in the heartlands of the Alentejo region, on the eastern side of Portugal, where some of the country's finest vineyards are located, and the sun shines 275 days a year. The 7.8-million-m^2 (!) estate has been in the same family for over 200 years and has played an essential role in the region. In the 19th century, they built an actual village on the estate where 50 families lived off the shared profit of the wine, olives, and vegetables they produced here. Children went to school on the estate, and there was even a bullfighting arena, which was considered a fun after-school activity in those days. José António Uva is the eighth-generation owner. His family's story inspired him to convert the estate into a contemporary hotel, restaurant and spa, where guests enjoy five-star luxury without losing sight of the property's history. In fact, as a guest, you are invited to become part of it, picking grapes during the harvest season, riding off into the sunset on a horse to see how vast the estate is, or gazing at the star-studded sky after dark on the arena where the bee hives once stood. This part of the Alentejo is the first site to be internationally certified as a Starlight Tourism Destination because there is little to no light pollution, and you have the best chance of seeing all the stars in the dark sky. The family set about transforming the estate with Eduardo Souto de Moura, the Portuguese architect who won the influential Pritzker Prize in 2011. An ivy-covered restaurant with sweeping views (also open to non-guests), a shop selling local products, a bar where you can try the wine that is produced on-site, a spa whose soft colour palette invites you to relax, and a choice of various suites and cottages. The smallest rooms are quite large and have a relaxing sofa and terrace. Families are in for even more of a treat. The Barn Cottage sleeps six and has three bedrooms, a kitchen and a spacious living room. They organise various activities for children here, such as a treasure hunt, or they can help build a bird's nest. Meanwhile, parents can relax and read a book by one of the two swimming pools or venture out to the medieval village of Monsaraz.

DESIGN STAYS

BEST ROOM:
All the suites overlook Monsaraz and have a living room with a comfortable sofa and a free-standing bathtub.

NEARBY:
Picturesque Monsaraz sits high on a mountain. On a clear day, you can see all the way to Spain.

TAKE HOME:
Barrocal's wildflower honey. Extra nice if you have followed the beekeeping workshop, where you learn why bees are so important and how they make honey.

SUSTAINABLE EFFORTS:
During the conversion, 250,000 (!) roof tiles from the old farms were preserved and recycled to construct the newer buildings.

FROM 350 euro A NIGHT

www.barrocal.pt

Monsaraz
Portugal

SÃO LOURENÇO DO BARROCAL

(COUNTRYSIDE)

Marqí
Colares, Portugal

204

Sometimes life can take a strange turn. One day, you have a successful fashion label in Copenhagen, then you discover a passion for photography, and next thing you know, you find yourself in Portugal because you've taken up surfing, only to open a hotel on the coast north of Lisbon with friends. It's just part of the life story of Mikkel Kristensen, who is happy to share the story of the house he found. Usually, hotel owners tend to completely refurbish an old property, with or without an architect, but this house already had tons of character, which Kristensen decided to preserve as is, accentuating it with mid-century modern furniture. Originally, this was the holiday home of a successful civil engineer who liked spending weekends here with friends and family, lounging around the pool or even dancing in the disco he had built in the house, which dates from the 80s. In any case there were plenty of rooms, seeing that these days the four floors hold eight hotel rooms. Some rooms give out onto the garden, while others are higher up in the building and have panoramic views. This is the case for the Deluxe Balcony Double where you can enjoy the sound of the singing birds from the terrace and gaze at the ever-changing skies. Marqí is near Praia Grande, a vast sandy beach. You can sometimes even see clouds drifting into the green valley from the balcony, which also overlooks the pool below, where the handsome clientèle likes to pose for a photo session. The communal living room and dining room, where breakfast is served – inside or outside on the terrace in the sun – are on the ground floor. Kristensen has succeeded in creating a casual atmosphere that makes it easy to strike up a conversation. Early in the morning, surfer guests set off together to the most beautiful beaches, while guests who love vintage cars admire the Mercedes in the driveway. At the communal table people share their favourite tips for the area over a tasty green risotto. You can easily walk to the beach, where there are several beach clubs, and one of the largest saltwater pools in Europe.

BEST ROOM:
The Deluxe Balcony Double has great views, and the energising Red Garden Room opens onto the garden.

NEARBY:
Praia Grande for a beach walk and Portugal's best surf spots.

FROM
120 euro
A NIGHT

www.marqi.holiday
Estrada do Rodízio 86
Colares

(COUNTRYSIDE)

Casa Mãe
Lagos, Portugal

BEST ROOM:

One of the Cabanas with a bath, private patio and hammock.

NEARBY:

Specialty coffee and brunch at Black & White in Lagos. And the surrounding beaches; Praia da Dona Ana for example is definitely a highlight.

TAKE HOME:

Oliófora created an essential oil for the hotel, inspired by the scents from Casa Mãe's garden. You can smell it throughout the hotel and can buy it in their shop.

SUSTAINABLE EFFORTS:

All skincare products are made without parabens and sulphates, using natural ingredients only, including cold-pressed almond oil from Amarante, a village in northern Portugal known for its wine and almonds.

Quitting your job as an investment banker in Paris and moving to Portugal is quite something, yet that is precisely what Veronique Polaert did. Since she didn't know anybody when she arrived, she decided to organise a pop-up dinner to meet new people, and that's how she was introduced to several Portuguese locals who were reviving their (grand) parents' crafts. Some of them made furniture, others weaved rugs, or created beautiful vases. Polaert had always dreamt of opening a hotel, and she found the stories of these makers so inspiring that she decided to bring the two worlds together. And that is how Casa Mãe was born. Whereas many hotels tend to use the same international design brands, at Casa Mãe you immediately notice the fresh selection of local designs you will not have seen anywhere else. Art by SÖNMUN, aromatic candles by Casa Bohemia and wall hangings by Rudimi. In the restaurant, they also work with local products where possible, mainly sourced from their mountain farm and from local farmers at the market. Lagos has always been a fishing village, so the fish doesn't get any fresher than this. A popular tourist destination, it is also the perfect base to explore the west of the Algarve. The coastline here is breathtaking, so the rocks surrounding sandy beaches and clear blue water are a popular feature in campaigns promoting Portugal as a tourist destination. Lagos is surrounded by a historic city wall that was built in the 15th century to protect it against pirates, and Casa Mãe is right next to it. So when you step out to the large terrace with your welcome drink, there is no avoiding it. From here, you also get a good idea of the hotel's layout in three different locations. The main building consists of spacious rooms in a peaceful colour scheme with a freestanding bath and a hammock on the balcony. The garden leads to the more spacious Cabanas, or bungalows, with a private terrace, outdoor shower and hammock. And then there is the more classically furnished manor house. You'll also spot the pool, spa and shop. Another lovely feature of the hotel are the workshops it organises: consider taking a cooking workshop, making ceramics, or going ocean fishing.

CASA MÃE

www.casamae.com
Rua do Jogo
da Bola 41
Lagos
DESIGN STAYS
FROM
185 euro
A NIGHT

215   CASA MÃE

(CITY)

Santa Clara 1728

Lisbon, Portugal

BEST ROOM:
Suite Santa Clara (70 m²) boasts a lovely armchair to read in and views over the Tagus River.

NEARBY:
The famous Feira da Ladra flea market is on the hotel's doorstep. The panoramic vantage points and narrow streets through which the iconic tram runs are just a short walk from the hotel.

SUSTAINABLE EFFORTS:
The ingredients used at Ceia are sourced from their own farm.

DON'T MISS:
Santa Fé is an old, refurbished boat you can book for a two-hour cruise on the Tagus.

João Rodrigues is a pilot flying around the world, but he is also the owner of five of Portugal's finest holiday homes and hotels. It all started in 2010 with Casas na Areia in Comporta. Originally the holiday home of the Rodrigues family, they soon decided they wanted to share the magic of this place – besides the main building there are three other houses – with others. Their architect Manuel Aires Mateus designed all four houses so that their origin comes alive through the materials, with references to history and a view of the surrounding, pristine nature. The main building, with a living room, kitchen and sand floor, was so unique that it soon began to be featured in magazines and blogs. After Casas na Areia, they refurbished two fishermen's cottages (Cabanas no Rio), an enchanting estate (Casa no Tempo), a lakeside house in the Alentejo (Casa na Terra), and a stately hotel in the heart of Lisbon (Santa Clara 1728). As with the country houses, Rodrigues and Aires Mateus wanted to offer guests a sense of stillness, this time in the city. The 18th-century palace has six spacious suites that exude a warm minimalist style. Here too, it's about letting the high-quality, locally manufactured materials speak for themselves, in combination with the amazing light that falls in through the large windows, with the colour palette changing depending on the time of day. The building's history has also been preserved: the ground floor and staircase are limestone, like the bathtubs. The hotel has a sheltered garden on the ground floor and a dining room with a large communal wooden dining table where guests can have breakfast. The table gives the hotel the look of a family home, a vibe they sought to create in all their locations. Rodrigues and his family live on the property's top two floors, and he will happily sit down and share his love for Portugal with guests. At Santa Clara 1728, it feels like you're staying with friends rather than in a hotel. In the evening, the dining room is transformed into Ceia, an intimate restaurant where 14 guests can taste various dishes made with ingredients sourced from the family's own farm, Casa no Tempo. It's located on a *herdade* (a 400-hectare estate), which has been in the family for generations. It also has an extensive vegetable garden where they grow vegetables, fruit, and herbs.

FROM 500 euro A NIGHT

www.silentliving.pt
Campo de Santa Clara 128
Lisbon
<< DESIGN STAYS >>

SANTA CLARA 1728

221 SANTA CLARA 1728

(COUNTRYSIDE)

Pa.te.os
Melides, Portugal

222

Melides is 130 kilometres south of Lisbon, a little further south than posh Comporta. In recent years, the latter has been in the spotlight because of its impressive holiday villas and the celebrities and royal families who like to holiday there. However, attention is gradually shifting to Melides, where Christian Louboutin recently opened a hotel, and the extensive Melides Art attracts artists and designers. Everyone agrees that the resort's unspoilt nature has a reinvigorating effect: the vastness of the beach, the star-studded sky overhead, and the olive grove, which is perfect for people who love horse riding. Sofia and Miguel

Charters, an enterprising couple from Lisbon, bought a piece of land there, built a holiday home, and initially intended to add four homes for their children. They asked architect Manuel Aires Mateus for his ideas, and he proposed four concrete houses where the inside and outside blend seamlessly. Hence the name 'Pa.*te*.os', a reference to patios. After receiving planning permission, they set to work. Although the houses look massive on the outside – with a playful twist whereby the roof is the same shape as the window in it – every room in the house has a door that leads outside. In Casa 4 (which is the house you see in the photographs), the living room opens out to a terrace with expansive views of the nature out front, the kitchen opens onto a large courtyard garden with a dining table and lounge bed, the bedroom opens out to a sheltered terrace and the bathroom opens out to yet another courtyard garden with an outdoor shower. That way, it's like a second room is tacked onto every room. The effect was so stunning that the Charters decided to turn the houses into a hotel. Or rather, four very exclusive holiday homes with hotel service. A scrumptious breakfast is delivered at a time of your choice, and you can also book a massage or yoga class. The masseuse or instructor will simply come to your casa. The estate also has a swimming pool you share with the guests in the other three houses. Although you might not want to leave your house: the view automatically compels you to slow down. Walking barefoot over the soft concrete makes you feel grounded and relaxed after a warm bath.

BEST ROOM:
Casa 4 is the second smallest house, but with 95m^2, it is the ideal holiday home for a couple. If there are four or six of you, Casa 1 and 2 are a good match.

NEARBY:
Horse riding at sunset on the beach at Melides, which can be booked through Passeios a Cavalo.

TAKE HOME:
British Lyn Harris of Perfumer H created a signature fragrance, especially for the hotel.

SUSTAINABLE EFFORTS:
The landscape is planted with plants that self-propagate to attract bees so they can make their own honey in the future.

FROM 650 euro A NIGHT

www.pateos.pt

Melides

(CITY)

Tipografia do Conto

Porto, Portugal

228

Tipografia do Conto is the second hotel project of the owners of Casa do Conto. Their first hotel suffered an unfortunate fate, opening in 2008 only to go up in flames one year later. Thankfully, they could fully restore the hotel and pay homage again to the typical 19th-century domestic architecture of Porto, which is especially noticeable in the historic granite façade and the new concrete stairwells and ceilings. Another striking feature are the Portuguese texts about the city in the ceiling by several local authors. Architecture lovers have been coming here for years. In 2019, they added a new chapter to this story with a second hotel, just a four-minute walk from the first one, in the Cedofeita district. And at Tipografia do Conto, the architecture also stands out. Here, too, they used a lot of concrete and have texts in the ceiling, but the design feels much warmer thanks to the wooden window and façade structures, mid-century modern furniture, and plants throughout. The building formerly housed a typography and graphic arts workshop, which explains the hotel's name and theme. This is reflected in the texts on the ceilings, the many books throughout the hotel, and the sleek design of their business card. Although it is a large building, the hotel has only ten rooms. The cheapest room has a lovely rooftop terrace, while the rooms around the patio have the same warm accents as the wooden façade. The downside here is that you can look into your neighbour's rooms across the patio. The hotel's secret asset, however, can be found outside. At first, it seems like there is just a small garden behind the building, but if you walk a little further, you will see the swimming pool. A great place to read, swim a few laps after a day in the city or simply enjoy the birdsong. The hotel also has a restaurant, but there are lots of great restaurants, shops and galleries to choose from in the creative Cedofeita district where it is situated. Early Cedofeita comes highly recommended for lunch. Its owners are also the founders of Early Made, a clothing shop in the same neighbourhood where they only sell brands made in Portugal. You can rent a bike from the hotel, which will get you to Casa da Música, a famous concert hall designed by Rem Koolhaas's OMA, in just five minutes.

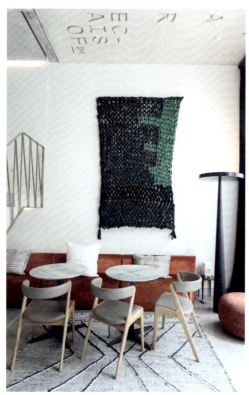

BEST ROOM:
The spacious A5 Suite Penthouse has its own sofa and desk. The room in the photos is the small B4 Suite Rooftop, with a balcony and unobstructed views.

NEARBY:
Época serves a simple but very good lunch.

231 TIPOGRAFIA DO CONTO

FROM
160 euro
A NIGHT

www.casadoconto.com
Rua de Álvares Cabral 28 Porto

232 DESIGN STAYS

CITY

Parkhotel Mondschein

Bolzano, Italy

234

Bolzano is the capital of South Tyrol, Italy's northernmost province, best known for its wine, nature, culinary culture, and wellness, combining all the flair of Italy with the grandeur of Austria. In Bolzano, the streets are lined with pastel-coloured buildings, with restaurants, shops and, above all, ice-cream parlours, but where the mountains are never out of sight. The building that houses Parkhotel Mondschein dates from 1330 and stands out with its orange façade and Art Nouveau-style balconies framed by ivy. The hotel is adjacent to a small park, and its terrace attracts locals and tourists who like to pause for a glass of wine or a snack on the green garden chairs by Hay. Every Wednesday evening in summer, the park transforms into an outdoor cinema. As the sun sets, they screen Italian classics here, including *La Grande Bellezza* and *Il tè nel deserto*. During the day, you can read on one of the red and white striped lounge chairs or enjoy the relaxing sound of birdsong. The hotel was recently acquired by ALTO, a local hotel group run by brothers Klaus and Moritz Dissertori, whose portfolio also includes 1477 Reichhalter, Hotel Schwarzschmied, and Villa Arnica in Lana. Together with Studio Biquadra, they have modernised the hotel without losing sight of its history. Their starting point was the 1960s, more specifically this period in Italian cinema, as you can tell in the rooms by a velvet sofa, lovely pink-and-burgundy bedside lamps, and a record player in the corner. The bar is like a film set, with its comfy armchairs, thick curtains, and art on the wall. Anyone drinking their first

coffee of the day here will immediately remem-ber why they came to Italy in the first place. Here, you won't find a hyped-up coffee concept with a long list of options. Instead, they serve an extremely good americano, made with beans from a local coffee roastery. If, after a good night's sleep (thanks to the thick blackout curtains) and a long hot bath, you want to start your day on less of a caffeine high, check out the yoga studio Arise on the ground floor. They offer a wide range of classes, from Slow Yoga Flow to Power Yoga. Bolzano is an excellent base for exploring the Dolomites, a Unesco World Heritage Site. People head into the mountains in summer for a hike, while winters draw winter sports enthusiasts.

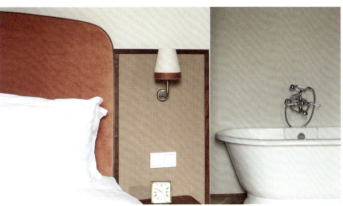

Piavestrasse 15
Bolzano
www.parkhotelmondschein.com

FROM
240
euro
A NIGHT

BEST ROOM:
The Grand Suite has a tub on legs, a sitting area, and a spacious bathroom with natural light.

NEARBY:
The Strada del Vino winds its way past the region's best wineries. Tip: use the Raisin app to find some independent natural winemakers.

TAKE HOME:
Mondschein's keychains, co-designed with A Kind of Guise.

DON'T MISS:
Start the day with a few laps in the outdoor pool.

DESIGN STAYS

(COUNTRYSIDE)

Villa Arnica

Lana, Italy

BEST ROOM:
The Suite has a bathtub on legs and is the most romantic option. The photos were taken in the Junior Suite, which is also highly recommended.

NEARBY:
1477 Reichhalter is an excellent place for lunch or dinner.

TAKE HOME:
The iconic yellow-and-white-striped bath towels.

SUSTAINABLE EFFORTS:
The hotel grows vegetables in Arnica Acker, a 3,000-m² kitchen garden.

South Tyrol in northern Italy is known for its nature, wellness, fine wine and gastronomy. The Dolomites are a Unesco World Heritage Site, attracting skiers and snowboarders in winter, while the mountainous area around Merano holds many surprises like palm trees and Art Nouveau buildings. Time seems to have ground to a standstill here, but in a good way, something that those in the know were quick to pick up on. The founder of Monocle magazine had a holiday home here, which explains why Merano also has its own Monocle store, and entrepreneurial brothers Klaus and Moritz Dissertori have since opened several hotels and restaurants in the area. Born in South Tyrol, they left to pursue international careers, only to return and breathe new life into the Hotel Schwarzschmied in Lana: the family already owned the hotel, but it was somewhat outdated. Nowadays, it is both a hotel and spa that also offers yoga classes. Other assets in the brothers' portfolio include Parkhotel Mondschein in Bolzano (see p. 234) and the highly recommended restaurant (and guesthouse) 1477 Reichhalter, also in Lana. And then there is Villa Arnica, a 1920s villa with just ten rooms and suites, for adults only. It feels like you're visiting family with creaky wooden floors, relaxing music from the antique speaker, an honesty bar, and many coffee table books in the alcoves. The suite is spacious with a bedroom, living room with a sofa and armchair, bathroom, and views of the town's picturesque church. A large garden surrounds the villa, where you can read your book in peace. The swimming pool, with its yellow and white loungers and parasols, looks like the set for a scene from a 1960s movie. Breakfast is served in the adjoining pool house with wicker chairs, wooden tables, and tropical plants and includes freshly squeezed juices and oatmeal with fruit. They also offer yoga classes in the morning and evening in the greenhouse, tucked away in a corner near the kitchen garden. This is also the case at the Hotel Schwarszchmied, which you can access through a gate. You can also go for a swim there or book a spa treatment. If you want to leave the villa, just take a walk into the authentic village for a tasty lunch or dinner at 1477 Reichhalter. Then, hop on the cable car five minutes up the road and head into the mountains for a walk with a view.

245 VILLA ARNICA

(COUNTRYSIDE)

Masseria Moroseta

Ostuni, Italy

A five-minute drive takes you from the photogenic town of Ostuni in Puglia through a landscape full of olive trees to the entrance of Masseria Moroseta. A *masseria* is a farmhouse with space for a few rooms, but its core business is to produce organic extra virgin olive oil, up to 2,000 litres a year in this case. The masseria has five hectares of land that you can see from the white main house, which is slightly elevated. But that's not all: in front of the olive trees is a swimming pool, and you can even see the sea in the distance. During the day, the sky changes colour in a picturesque way, which, together with the architecture of the masseria, results in a beautiful spectacle, especially at sunset. That was one of the main reasons owner Carlo Lanzini fell in love with the place, hiring his best friend Andrew Trotter to take care of the architecture, interior and landscape design. Trotter is the co-founder of Open House Magazine. After years of publishing articles about the most beautiful houses, Masseria Moroseta was his first own project. He now divides his time between Spain and Italy and has since designed many properties, including holiday homes and hotels such as Villa Cardo and Borgo Gallana. Moroseta came about sustainably: its one-metre thick walls mean it is so well insulated that it needs very little air conditioning in summer and has a pleasant indoor climate in winter. The six rooms, two suites, and four classic rooms are all arranged around the courtyard with long dining tables and vines above the doors, creating a community vibe: after wandering around the house open-mouthed, guests naturally tend to gather around the dining table and exchange (travel) stories over freshly baked biscuits. Food connects, something Italians know all too well, which is why chef Giorgia Eugenia Goggi likes to pamper guests with a sumptuous dinner or a cooking workshop. Breakfast is always seasonal with fresh fruit, freshly baked cake, and a *frise*, a typical Puglian sandwich with mozzarella and various types of tomatoes. The ingredients are sourced from their own vegetable garden, and the food is presented on tableware from the region. There is no need to leave a hotel like Masseria Moroseta, and who would want to, as the pool and lounge chairs beckon, inviting you to indulge in some reading. That said, there is plenty to explore: you can visit hilltop Ostuni, they organise yoga retreats at the masseria, and you can explore Puglia's beaches – which have been compared to the Maldives – on the hotel's own boat.

BEST ROOM:
The suite has a sitting room, bedroom, and spacious patio.

NEARBY:
Borgo Antico bistro is a bar in Ostuni with several floors and excellent views.

TAKE HOME:
Their own extra virgin olive oil.

SUSTAINABLE EFFORTS:
The living room has windows on both sides, eliminating the need for air conditioning.

GOOD TO KNOW:
Non-guests are also welcome to join for dinner.

www.masseriamoroseta.it
Contrada Lamacavallo
Ostuni

FROM 300 euro A NIGHT

250 DESIGN STAYS

COUNTRYSIDE

The Wild Hotel

Mykonos, Greece

Once upon a time, the so-called 'Wild Ones' lived in this small fishing village. These fishermen were not afraid of anything or anyone, braving even the wildest seas to supply the island with fish. The Wild Hotel pays tribute to these men. From the lounger with pink cushions by the infinity pool, you look out over the bay from where they set out on their wild voyages. Now a sailboat bobs there, and the sunsets are more than photoworthy. Greek restaurateur Nikos Valveris opened Interni Restaurant & Bar on Mykonos more than 20 years ago. It continues to be a popular nightlife spot with an interior designed by Italian designer Paola Navone. In 2019, Valveris's sons continued the family's love affair with the Greek island, opening The Wild Hotel. A luxury boutique hotel for people who like peace, privacy and bohemian interiors. There are 40 rooms and suites. Some have garden views, but most overlook the sea from a terrace or private (plunge) pool. The room interiors are warm and welcoming, with lots of wood, rattan and beige hues, and this is echoed throughout the rest of the hotel: in the reception area, the poolside bar and The Taverna, a fuss-free restaurant serving authentic Greek food with a modern twist.

At RAW, the hotel's second restaurant, nestled in the rocks, guaranteeing privacy and panoramic views, the menu includes all kinds of raw delights inspired by Japanese and Mediterranean cuisine – expect sushi and seafood. During the day, you can listen to relaxing music by the infinity pool and order a tasty cocktail or snacks from the café. The Wild Hotel is unique, however, in that it has its own private beach. Just the place for a cooling dip in the crystalline blue water, and they also have bar service. No need to roll out your own towel; sunbeds with parasols await. Swimming is a great way to burn off all that delicious moussaka you ate, but the hotel also has an outdoor gym. Burpees will feel like much less of a slog with a view like this, especially if you can take a refreshing outdoor shower or book a massage afterwards.

BEST ROOM:
The Signature Suite with plunge pool and sea view.

NEARBY:
Dinner at Noema in Mykonos Town (20-minute drive).

SUSTAINABLE EFFORTS:
They work with as many local ingredients as possible in their restaurants.

DON'T MISS:
The hydrotherapy waterfall in the Quiet Zone spa.

FROM **295** euro A NIGHT

Kalafatis, Loulos Agia Anna
Mykonos
www.thewildhotel.com

THE WILD HOTEL

257   THE WILD HOTEL

(COUNTRYSIDE)

Parīlio

Paros, Greece

258

Two huge boulders in the pool: it's a striking feature in the otherwise perfectly landscaped hotel where the space between two sunbeds seems precisely the same almost everywhere. However, the rocks are a reference to the mountains in the distance. Whether you take a swim in the morning or gaze at the sunset in the evening, the landscape, and therefore the hotel, changes throughout the day as the sun's brightness varies. A connection you can sense throughout the hotel, which also explains its name. Parīlio is an amalgamation of Paros and *ilios*, the Greek word for sun. It is also sometimes described as the aura of the sun. Kalia and Antonis Eliopoulos run several hotels, including Istoria on Santorini, and collaborated with Stamos Hondrodimos of Interior Design Laboratorium on Parīlio. He was inspired by the surrounding nature and the traditional Greek villages with their snow-white houses (these are the hotel's suites), which are connected, resembling a monastery. When you walk from one of the suites to the restaurant, in the open air, your pace imperceptibly slows, and you soon realise that you are whispering. Guests flock here for the nature and tranquillity or they can seek out the hustle and bustle in one of the nearby beaches or villages. At Parīlio, they were adamant about working with artisans for the many ceramics throughout the hotel and the wall hangings above the beds. These

were inspired by the hotel's view of the cliffs at Koukounaries, where one of the Aegean coast's oldest and most significant acropolis structures has been discovered. The 33 suites have a wall hanging by LRNCE, some have a private pool and others a comfortable armchair. The restaurant, Mr E, is named after the hotel's owner. Chef Alexandros Tsiotinis, who previously worked at Le Bristol in Paris, has put together a menu of Greek and Mediterranean dishes, such as grilled squid or a vegetarian orzo with aubergine. The Elios Spa is a holistic wellness spot where you can pamper your body and face with special treatments using products from Greek apothecary Korres. For the Signature Massage, they use an aromatic oil of your choice, ensuring your body will feel reborn in just under an hour.

www.pariliohotelparos.com
Kolymbithres, Naoussa
Paros
<< DESIGN STAYS >>

FROM
350 euro
A NIGHT

BEST ROOM:
The Uranus Suite has a hot tub and panoramic views.

NEARBY:
Kolymbithres Beach and the photogenic village of Naoussa, with its many restaurants and shops.

TAKE HOME:
One of the ceramic bowls or plates in their on-site shop The Anthologist.

SUSTAINABLE EFFORTS:
They use an innovative water filtration system that purifies local tap water by extracting the impurities but retains the essential salts and minerals, resulting in very high-quality water.

(COUNTRYSIDE)

Casa Cook

Samos, Greece

In 2016, Casa Cook opened its first hotel in Rhodes, a small adults-only boutique hotel with a bohemian vibe. In the following years, they added more hotels to their line-up, including in Egypt, Mykonos and Samos. The latter was designed by the architects of Greek studio Block 722, who also created other acclaimed design hotels in Greece such as Olea All Suite and Meraviglia Slow Living. For Casa Cook Samos, the team looked to the Greek island for inspiration; the colours of the ceramics they found there, for example, formed the starting point for the hotel's colour palette. They wanted the resort to feel like a Greek village, so instead of high-rise buildings, you'll find almost all rooms are on the ground floor. To create a community vibe all the rooms are arranged around several swimming pools, so it's inviting to strike up a conversation with your neighbours. But

privacy is an important aspect in the hotel too. Some suites have a private pool and there's a villa with several sun beds and a large swimming pool. The adults-only resort is actually divided into two parts: the majority of the rooms are located in one part and then, across the quiet street, there's the Beach House. This is where the lavish breakfast is served in the morning, but the restaurant is open all day for snacks, lunch, dinner and more. In front of the restaurant is the pebble beach with its loungers for hotel guests who want to take a nap in the sun or read a book in the shade under an umbrella. The sea water here feels wonderfully pleasant if you want to cool off – from June to September, temperatures hover around 30 degrees. The hotel also has a spa where guests can book a wide range of body and facial treatments. And every morning at 8.30 am, you can take a free yoga class in the Yoga Shala. Samos itself is a welcoming island, best known as the birthplace of Pythagoras and the Greek goddess Hera, and for its sweet dessert wine.

CASA COOK

Potokaki
Samos

FROM
220 euro
A NIGHT

BEST ROOM:

The Swim Up Suite. These suites have a private terrace from where you can take a dip in the communal pool to cool down.

NEARBY:

Pythagorion is a typical Greek village. Stop at Pergamonto for dinner and visit a free exhibition at Art Space Pythagorion in the evening.

TAKE HOME:

The ceramics in the hotel shop are made by local artists. The shop also carries a design version of the Pythagoras cup, a typical souvenir from Samos.

SUSTAINABLE EFFORTS:

The hotel uses as little plastic as possible, there are solar panels on the roof, and a circular water purification system makes sure not too much water is wasted for the pools.

CASA COOK

Pauline Egge is the owner of **Petite Passport**, a travel platform for design lovers. She launched her site in 2010 and since then has been posting weekly updates about the world's most beautiful places to eat, shop and stay. She has also built a vibrant Instagram community with more than 110k followers. In 2015, she self-published her first city guides of Amsterdam, Barcelona, Berlin, and Paris, which led to a series of 11 regularly updated guides and two magazines. Nowadays, she still travels the world to find the most inspiring places for her readers, in addition to giving talks and advice on travel and hotel trends, and collaborating with companies such as The Hoxton Hotels and various tourism boards to create custom-made guides and content.

Design Stays readers get a one-month free trial for the membership-based website and access to a database of more than 1,400 articles, as well as tips for places to go near the hotels in this book. Use the 'designstay' coupon code to unlock your free month-long trial*

```
* The membership can be terminated at any
  time with a notice period of 30 days. After
  the trial it is automatically renewed, and
  you will be billed 9.99 euros per month.
```

Thank *you* for reading this book.

Whether leafing through *Design Stays* has inspired you to plan a trip, you have already stayed at some of the hotels recommended on my website, or own the whole series of Petite Passport Guides, it's your enthusiasm that has allowed me to do what I love most these past 14 years: curate lists of the most inspiring places to go. Of course, none of this would be possible without all the entrepreneurs, designers, chefs, and other daredevils who grew the seed of an idea into something more so we can all enjoy it. Thank you!

Thanks to all the hoteliers in this book for their warm welcome, their stories and, of course, their dedication to offering their guests the best time of their lives. Thank you also to publisher Marc Verhagen who made my dream of creating a coffee table book come true. It is an honour to have found a place among your lovingly crafted and highly inspiring publications. Thank you to Yah-Leng Yu, Sylvester Tan, Yun Xuan Lee and Ying Xuan Loh of Foreign Policy Design, who have been Petite Passport's regular designers for over ten years. I got to know you through the business card you made for The Waterhouse at South Bund in Shanghai, after which we met up in Singapore, Barcelona and Rotterdam to forge plans for books and websites. I am in awe of your innovativeness, skill, and humour.

And, finally, thank you to everyone who has contributed to the making of this book, in particular Miranda Bruinzeel, Hadewijch Ceulemans, Sandy Logan, Katya Doms, Alexander Santos Lima, Eva Zahrawi Ruiz, Joost Verbraak, my family and friends, and my colleagues on the second floor of Het Industriegebouw.

love, Pauline

INSTAGRAM
INSTAGRAM.COM/
PETITEPASSPORT
FACEBOOK / PINTEREST
@PETITEPASSPORT
#PETITEPASSPORT

info@petitepassport.com
www.petitepassport.com